The Columbus Dispatch

FIGHT
TO THE END

OHIO STATE'S LEGENDARY RUN TO THE NATIONAL CHAMPIONSHIP

ADAM CAIRNS/COLUMBUS DISPATCH

THE LINEUP

Executive editor
Michael Shearer

Sports editor
Brian White

Assistant sports editor
Lori Schmidt

OSU beat reporters
Joey Kaufman
Bill Rabinowitz

Columnist
Rob Oller

Photo editor
Kyle Robertson

Photographers
Adam Cairns
Samantha Madar
Barbara J. Perenic
Kyle Robertson

Project coordinator
Gene Myers

Special thanks
Chris Thomas
Noah Amstadter
Clarissa Young
Josh Williams

**Content packaged
by Mojo Media, Inc.**
Joe Funk
Jason Hinman

ABOUT THE BOOK: *Fight to the End* condenses a year's worth of the world's best coverage of the Ohio State Buckeyes from the *Columbus Dispatch*. Follow the Buckeyes at dispatch.com and with a print subscription at 888-884-9026. The book includes coverage from the USA TODAY Network, which includes the *Dispatch*.

TRIUMPHBOOKS**.COM**
⬛ 𝕏 ⬛ @TRIUMPHBOOKS

814 North Franklin Street
Chicago, Illinois 60610
Phone: (312) 337-0747

FIGHT TO THE END

ADAM CAIRNS/COLUMBUS DISPATCH

4

THE CHAMPS

What happens when two of college football's most storied programs meet with the national championship on the line? History, as the Buckeyes topped the Fighting Irish for Ohio State's first title since 2014.

12

THE SEASON

In the first year of an expanded Big Ten, it was a season of highs and lows: A close loss at Oregon. Triumphs over fellow playoff qualifiers Penn State and Indiana. And a regular-season finale against Michigan that didn't go OSU's way.

90

THE GLORY

In the first 12-team College Football Playoff, it came down to four games to win the title — a first-round game against Tennessee at the Horseshoe, the Rose Bowl in Pasadena, the Cotton Bowl in Texas, and then, finally, the CFP title game in Atlanta.

THE CHAMPS

'ETCHED IN HISTORY'

This Ohio State Team is Most Deserving of All Buckeyes Champions

By Rob Oller • January 20, 2025

After it was over, after the confetti fell and the cigars were lit, the intoxicating fragrance of Ohio State history wafted through the Buckeyes' locker room in Mercedes-Benz Stadium, mixing with the smell of burning tobacco.

Sophomore safety Caleb Downs said it first. Senior guard Josh Fryar said it next. And once-upon-a-time tailback Maurice Clarett said it last: This OSU team, the one that defeated/survived/squeaked past — however you want to describe the 34-23 victory against Notre Dame in the College Football Playoff national championship game Jan. 20 at Atlanta — was the best ever.

"It was a serious climb, but I'm grateful for all the ups and downs because of the lessons we learned," Downs said, stogie hanging from his mouth, "National Champions" hat perched upon his head. "That's why we're here today."

And then ...

"We're the best."

The devil is in the definition, of course. What defines best? Most talented? Most dominant? Most beloved? All those things we can debate. But not this: Whether you believe the 2024 Buckeyes deserve to be labeled best ever, they absolutely should be crowned the most deserving champion in school history.

The other six OSU national champions are worthy of honor, but none had to navigate a meat-grinder playoff that saw the Buckeyes defeat four consecutive top-10 teams, culminating with the easy-until-it-wasn't victory over the Fighting Irish, who for a hot second conjured horrific images of past Ohio State agonies.

OSU turns back comeback

But what did you expect besides a double-digit win that was much closer? Much about this season felt like a frustrating fender bender for coach Ryan Day and the gang. Why should that change in a stadium named for a car company that brags about how well it survives crashes?

No, this title tilt played out exactly as it should have, with Ohio State fans whooping it up before nearly choking on their 2019 Clemson and 2022 Georgia, or, for older folks, their 1998 Michigan State and 1975 Southern Cal memories. (Say this for the Buckeyes, they seldom make things easy on their paying customers.) Anything other than a nail-biter would have felt too easy. Heaven forbid.

I mean, the Buckeyes were left for dead following the 13-10 loss to unranked Michigan. At least outside the walls of the Woody Hayes Athletic Center. Inside it, the believers believed. OK, so it took a come-to-Jesus meeting (the Buckeyes held hands and prayed at the end of it) to reverse what happened against the Wolverines. But that is not a negative, rather just another beautiful line in an epic poem of a season.

Quarterback Will Howard rose to the occasion during the Buckeyes' playoff run, ultimately earning the honor of top offensive player in college football's championship game. ADAM CAIRNS/COLUMBUS DISPATCH

After Michigan came Tennessee in Ohio Stadium, then the rematch with Oregon in the Rose Bowl, followed by a trip to Dallas to play Texas in its back 40. Not exactly the Sisters of the Poor we're talking about.

"It's gonna be etched in history," Fryar said of navigating a 16-game season that by the end felt more like 20, such was the weekly challenge of preparing for top-ranked teams. "The battles in our heads. The injuries. It's not for me to say if we're the best in history, but the stuff we've been through? Yeah, I would say so."

Finally, there was Clarett, whose own redemption ties in nicely with these Buckeyes having risen from the Michigan loss to win the seventh natty in school history, joining 1942, 1954, 1957, 1968, 2002 and 2014. (Ohio State also claims 1961 and 1970, but those teams were honored by the Football Writers Association of America and National Football Foundation, not the more established Associated Press and UPI/coaches polls.)

Clarett was one of the key cogs in the 2002 title team, and he is not about to undercut his former teammates by saying this year's team is better at football than his was.

But the 41-year-old, who over the past 15 years has turned his life around after making a mess of it in his mid-20s, is not shy about declaring his admiration for the team that just beat Notre Dame.

How OSU hung together

"I love these guys equally as much (as the 2002 team)," Clarett said, standing outside the winning locker room. "But for a different significance. This team means more to me as an adult, because you have to understand the emotion, adversity, the human element. When I look at the on-field play of the players, I don't care about that. I'm talking about the character of the guys and all the (expletive) they've been through. What you see here is perseverance in action. They didn't beat just nobodies.

Running back Quinshon Judkins celebrates with teammates after scoring one of his three touchdowns against Notre Dame. The Ole Miss transfer had two TDs rushing and one receiving.
ADAM CAIRNS/COLUMBUS DISPATCH

"After you've been publicly beat up, and I know a lot about that, when I say these dudes mean a lot to me it's from a personal life standpoint. You start out with all these expectations and you fail publicly and get criticized horribly, as Ryan did, and you turn the corner and redeem yourself. That's what is special to me."

Is this the best Ohio State team ever? Who knows? The Super Sophs of 1968 were damn impressive. The 2002 Buckeyes were tough as nails and the 2014 edition beat Alabama. Nuff said. I can't speak for 1942, 1954 and 1957, but I wouldn't bet against them.

But the Buckeyes who just beat Notre Dame are the greatest in their own way. They fell off the mountain, got back up and scaled it to the summit. That legacy is hard to beat and will never go up in smoke. Cigar or otherwise. ■

Opposite: Ohio State wasn't perfect in the 2024 season, but it earned its spot in the pantheon of the program's greatest teams. ADAM CAIRNS/ COLUMBUS DISPATCH

Above: Ohio State coach Ryan Day persisted through public backlash and job speculation to lead the Buckeyes to their first national championship in a decade, and maybe their sweetest. ADAM CAIRNS/COLUMBUS DISPATCH

THE SEASON

CALLING THEIR SHOTS

Ohio State Must Beat Michigan and Win Natty to Appease Restless Natives

By Rob Oller • August 28, 2024

For the first time since before World War II, Ohio State won't have to cross a minefield to win a national championship. Instead of the dreaded misstep blowing up their title chances — think Iowa in 2017 and Purdue in 2018 — the Buckeyes can suffer a bad loss and live to see another day. They even can lose twice and probably still get in the new 12-team playoff.

Welcome to the NFL, folks.

A history lesson: Prior to 1936, a hodgepodge of unofficial media polls and mathematical ratings systems crowned yearly national champions. In 1935, for example, 8-0 Minnesota finished No. 1 in some polls, No. 2 in others and No. 5 in another. Ohio State (7-1) ranked anywhere from No. 4 to No. 8. Associated Press sports editor Alan Gould ranked Minnesota, Princeton and SMU in a three-way tie for No. 1.

Because a spread-the-wealth mentality ruled at that time, rankings were not the end-all, be-all like they are today. Likewise, losing one game did not spell disaster.

It was not until the arrival of the weekly AP rankings in 1936 when one-and-done became a thing. A lone loss did not automatically kill your hopes of winning a mythical poll national championship, but it did put your chances on life support. And two losses pulled the plug.

That all changes this season, when the expanded playoff means even two losses will not necessarily ruin a run to the national championship.

That stress-reducing reality is Part I of the Ohio State narrative entering this season. The Buckeyes no longer have to win every game to feel safe. I will miss the gravity of every game being a must-win, but such is the evolution — or deconstruction — of an amateur sport that increasingly is being professionalized.

Part II of OSU's story has a touch of irony, because while the Buckeyes can lose two games and probably be fine, coach Ryan Day cannot lose one game and feel safe. If that game is Michigan.

Yes, I know, the Michigan game is big every year. But it's not every year when an OSU coach is looking to break an 0-3 streak against the Wolverines. Day is 1-3 against the Buckeyes' biggest rival, not quite John Cooper territory — Coop was 0-5-1 against UM before getting his first win as OSU's coach — but shaky enough that a fourth consecutive loss would further inflame his critics and lose him many current supporters.

Especially this season, when Michigan has only five starters returning from its national championship team, the Buckeyes need to beat Blue. I think they will, but I also thought they would win the past three matchups. Nostradamus I'm not.

The pressure was on coach Ryan Day and the Buckeyes to knock off the rival Wolverines again and ride the momentum to an elusive national championship. ADAM CAIRNS/COLUMBUS DISPATCH

But we're jumping too far ahead in the story. Remember, Part I is about facing an easier path to the College Football Playoff, not only because of the additional eight playoff spots available but because OSU's regular-season schedule is a relative breeze, with eight home games, including Michigan Nov. 30. The toughest tests are at Oregon (Oct. 12) and at Penn State (Nov. 2), but the Buckeyes can lose one of those, maybe both, and still make the playoff, depending on how the Big Ten championship game plays out.

What Ohio State cannot do is lose three games, or lose to Penn State and Michigan. If the latter happens, especially if Michigan has a few losses, the Buckeyes put their fate in the hands of the playoff selection committee, of which three members have strong Ohio ties (Jim Grove, Gary Pinkel and David Sayler) but also includes Michigan athletic director Warde Manuel. Is conference loyalty and financial windfall stronger than rivalry pettiness? You tell me.

Two sets of numbers:

- Day is 39-0 against unranked teams and should be 43-0 by the end of September, given that Akron, Western Michigan, Marshall and likely Michigan State will not be ranked at the time. After that, Day could end the season 47-0 if Nebraska, Purdue, Northwestern and Indiana remain unranked. Day's record streak — no other coach has begun a career by going 39-0 against unranked opponents — has to end at some point, but not this season.
- Day is 17-8 against ranked teams, but 2-5 against top-five competition and 1-2 against teams ranked higher than OSU at the time. As critics love to point out, he doesn't lose the little ones but can't win the big one.

Part II. Day has an estimated $20 million in name, image and likeness money at his disposal,

which so far has helped land the No. 2 recruiting class behind Alabama. He has offensive guru Chip Kelly calling plays. He has a top-five defense. He needs to beat Michigan. Or all the above is chaff.

We have yet to discuss these Buckeyes' strengths and weaknesses. When people ask how Ohio State will be, my stock answer is: "Really good." How's that for in-depth analysis? Seldom am I willing to predict anything extraordinary. Why? I have witnessed quiet teams make incredible noise (2002, 2014), watched so-so teams come on late (2014) and covered teams (2003, 2007, 2015) that spit the bit after being picked to cross the line first.

The 2024 Buckeyes look primed to win it all, but I'm taking a prove-it-to-me approach with the offensive line, and I want to see quarterback Will Howard win a close game (Penn State?) before signing off on the Kansas State transfer leading OSU to the promised land. Howard's ability to run gives him the edge on last year's B+ quarterback, Kyle McCord, who despite criticism went 11-1 as the starter, but can Howard make big throws in the biggest games? Stay tuned.

The Buckeyes offense should shine, and the defense will sparkle. Anything short of advancing to the playoff semifinals will shower disappointment on fans who assume OSU will reach the title game.

Two intriguing scenarios: What if Ohio State loses to Michigan but wins it all? Is Day safe? He should be. Or, conversely, if the Buckeyes break their three-game losing streak to the Maize and Blue but flame out before reaching the playoff semifinals? Keep Day, I say.

Taking the preseason pulse of Buckeye Nation, my sense is "Beat Michigan" is the fans' No. 1 mantra of 2024, even more important than 1a, which is beating Georgia/Texas/Alabama/Oregon/

One of the preseason highlights was the unveiling of a statue for former Ohio State Buckeyes running back Archie Griffin outside of Ohio Stadium. The statue commemorates the 50th anniversary of Griffin's two Heisman trophies. ADAM CAIRNS/COLUMBUS DISPATCH

etc. at the national championship game in Atlanta.

Ultimately, Part I and II play off each other. As OSU's softish schedule winds down, Michigan awaits like a long par-5 with water fronting a devilish green. First shot safe. Second shot safe. Hit the green in regulation. Slippery 20-footer for birdie. Good luck avoiding a three-putt bogey.

Michigan's season is starting off messy. The NCAA has spoken curses upon the Wolverines. Jim Harbaugh jumped ship and insists he will not lie, steal or cheat in the NFL. Connor Stalions is taking his spying scheme to Netflix. Coming off their national title run, the Wolverines are a bit fat and perhaps too happy.

The Game should be a relatively easy get for the Buckeyes. So why does beating Michigan feel more menacing than going deep into the playoff? Maybe because OSU has been prone to dropping turkeys during Thanksgiving week. For Day's sake, it better not happen again this season. ∎

SAFETY

CALEB DOWNS

The Making of Caleb Downs and the Mind that Could Elevate an Elite Ohio State Defense

By Joey Kaufman • August 30, 2024

Caleb Downs sat in a team meeting room in the Alabama football facility, waiting for coach Nick Saban to appear in front of the Crimson Tide players.

On the weekday afternoon in January, he expected Saban to outline the phases of the offseason program. Their season had ended nine days earlier with a loss to Michigan in a College Football Playoff semifinal.

Saban instead arrived with another message. He told them he was retiring, ending a legendary career that included six national championships in his tenure in Tuscaloosa.

"I didn't believe it at first," Downs said. "It was a shell-shocked moment."

All of the Alabama players tried to process the abrupt announcement. One freshman turned to a row of teammates asking whether Saban might be joking. The mere suggestion prompts Downs to chortle seven months later.

"That dude does not joke," Downs said.

Downs understood Saban's retirement as a possibility when he enrolled at Alabama a year earlier.

Saban, who turned 72 in October, was older than all other coaches in the Football Bowl Subdivision outside of North Carolina's Mack Brown, who is 73.

And Saban had been open about the fact that he would step down if he no longer felt he could elevate the program.

"He didn't lie to me during recruitment," Downs said.

Yet it was another thing to hear the words coming out of his mouth.

For nearly two decades, Saban was the king of college football who had built a modern dynasty at Alabama.

Players flocked to him. He held a particular appeal to safeties such as Downs, as his background was coaching defensive backs. He sat in on their position meetings. Downs likened him to Yoda, the wise Jedi master from the "Star Wars" movies, for his wealth of knowledge.

"He was probably the best coach of all-time," Downs said, "so I wanted to learn from him, wanted to be coached by him."

The decision would alter his career. In the aftermath of Saban's retirement, Downs put his name in the NCAA transfer portal and left for Ohio State in a span of weeks.

When he was the top-ranked high school safety in the nation in the class of 2023, Downs gave the Buckeyes a long look. He liked their winning

In addition to his physical talents, focus and preparation are keys to safety Caleb Downs' success.
ADAM CAIRNS/COLUMBUS DISPATCH

tradition and tight-knit locker room. Having grown up in a suburb of Atlanta, he also appreciated the school's location within a city.

But as he took a second glance, the makeup of the roster was especially difficult to ignore. The Buckeyes returned a loaded senior class on the defensive side of the ball with established veterans holding off on departing for the NFL.

The allure was apparent.

"It was a chance to be a part of a special year," Downs said.

Downs, an All-America as a freshman at Alabama, also figures to enhance Ohio State's star-studded defense, the backbone of its pursuit of its first national championship in a decade, starting with a precocious mind.

Brainpower behind path to stardom

Tanya Downs noticed her son's imagination as early as age 2.

Plastic football figures covered his bedroom floor at their home in northern Georgia. Caleb spent hours rearranging the pieces into teams lining up against each other.

"He had plays on offense and defense," she said. "He was like the coach and knew exactly where each player was supposed to be and why they were supposed to be there."

He continued leaving traces of his cerebral side.

By the time he joined a youth football league in Gwinnett County at age 6, he understood his team's defense so well that he would reposition linemen into their gaps at the line of scrimmage.

"You can see him moving his guys pre-snap," said his father, Gary Downs. "Or a kid comes in the game and he's putting the kid in the right spot on the field."

Genetics suggested he might have a high football IQ, a blend of his parents' experiences. Tanya is a high school calculus teacher. Gary is a former NFL running back who spent six years with the Atlanta Falcons, Denver Broncos and New York Giants.

But they saw Caleb's instincts on the field,

the ways in which he understood alignments and responsibilities, as more than inherited traits.

"That ability he has to do that has been there," Gary said. "That is a God-given ability that he has."

Caleb lined up most of the time at running back and linebacker until he enrolled at Mill Creek High School in 2019.

The Hawks' varsity team had a need at safety, prompting him to start early on, moving him to the back end.

The position made a natural fit. Safety enabled him to call plays and make checks, among other responsibilities. Once the ball was snapped, he was rarely isolated.

"It fits his personality," Mill Creek coach Josh Lovelady said. "There's action going on every play."

As he blossomed into a heralded recruit, Downs grew so advanced in diagnosing personnel that he called out offenses' plays before the snap. Opposing coaches, caught off guard by the practice, wondered whether the Hawks had stolen their play-calling signs until Lovelady leveled with them.

"There's a lot of coaches going, 'Damn, there's nothing more deflating than we're about to run a play and he already knows it,' " Lovelady said. "I'm like. 'Well, you've got to realize this is Caleb Downs.' "

Downs used the knowledge to redirect other defenders into better spots. Other times, it was for his own playmaking. He baited receivers into running specific routes, allowing him to blanket them in coverage. He has the range and athleticism needed to capitalize, too.

"He'll line himself in a position where it looks like there is no way he can cover that route," said Freeman Davis, who coaches the safeties at Mill Creek. "The moment you run it, he's running the route with you. He's notorious for that. That's the thing he is 100% great at."

It takes intuition, but Downs also puts in preparation. Davis estimated Downs would watch about 15 hours of film of opponents each week in high school, memorizing groupings.

A transfer from Alabama, Caleb Downs played a key role on Ohio State's terrific defense. Downs played free safety and returned punts. ADAM CAIRNS/COLUMBUS DISPATCH

He began following the strict routine as a freshman with the Hawks. Playing in Georgia's highest state classification, he knew a learning curve awaited.

"You've got to find ways to be confident on the field," Downs said. "You can't just have a random belief in yourself."

The dedication was apparent last year, when he emerged as a breakout star at Alabama, becoming the first freshman to lead the Crimson Tide in tackles.

Only three defenders in the Southeastern Conference in 2023 had more than Downs' 107 tackles.

"He just had this mentality and vibe about him that he was a veteran," said Seth McLaughlin, a fifth-year senior center who also transferred to Ohio State from Alabama. "I would call him 'big bro' even though he's four years younger than me because of the way he carried himself. I know I was joking, but it's a testament to how he goes about his work."

Downs' family experience

That work ethic had a model in an undersized slot receiver.

Josh Downs never grew as tall as his younger brother, reaching only 5-feet-9. But despite standing three inches shorter, he scraped his way to the NFL.

A third-round selection of the Indianapolis Colts last year, he set the franchise's rookie receptions record, breaking a 27-year-old mark once established by Marvin Harrison Sr.

"He worked and worked and worked," Gary Downs said, "and Caleb saw Josh."

The brothers began training together in elementary school. They ran hills in their neighborhood and worked out in their cul-de-sac.

"The neighbors would come out," Tanya Downs said, "and just be like, 'There goes the Downs boys.' "

As the routines expanded with age, and they were also joined by their older sister, Kameron Downs, who played soccer at Kennesaw State, Gary left them note cards with regimens to follow after school or between practices. Footwork drills. Jump rope. Balance pad.

If they were watching TV, they did pushups, sit-ups and lunges between commercials.

They continued on family vacations, finding any piece of grass or parking lot pavement near a hotel. Even during a trip last month to one of Florida's panhandle beaches for the Fourth of July holiday, they brought equipment.

Between an open field and the sand, they kept conditioning with an eye toward their respective training camps.

"Just like you bring the beach towels and the goggles and the snorkels," Gary said, "we're going to bring the bungees and the sleds and the balls."

Even Caleb's earliest football memories as a child include putting on pads and hitting Josh in their living room.

"It's definitely been very much of a family experience for me," he said.

Downs' road to Columbus

Ohio State held an advantage in recruiting Downs the second time around in January 2024.

His familiarity with the school afforded the staff an opportunity to dive further into X's and O's, tailoring their pitch to his inquisitive nature. They had gone over a host of other factors, as he had just taken an official visit a year and half earlier.

So when a traveling party including coach Ryan Day, defensive coordinator Jim Knowles, cornerbacks coach Tim Walton and safeties coach Matt Guerrieri met with Downs at his family's home the day after entering the portal, they dedicated their time to discussing his potential fit in the defense.

"Nothing else mattered," Guerrieri said. "It was football. It was about the system and what's the plan for him."

They laid out laptops on a coffee table in the living room. Over a course of four hours, the screens flashed video cutups from Downs' snaps as a freshman at Alabama to sequences of the Buckeyes' safeties over the past two seasons.

Caleb Downs celebrates a tackle during the early season win over Western Michigan.
ADAM CAIRNS/COLUMBUS DISPATCH

The variety allowed them to compare roles and responsibilities between schemes.

"This was like fine-tuned minutiae," Guerrieri said.

Gary Downs offered them all coffee and donuts not long after their arrival. He picked them up at a Starbucks. But it took a while until they budged from the couches. Caleb's eyes were glued to the film.

"He was locked in," Gary said. "I don't think he moved."

Between clips, Caleb probed them about a range of situations, the calls to counteract a check by a quarterback or responses in the red zone. No detail was too granular.

He wondered as well about the assignments for other positions, seeking a broader base of knowledge of Knowles' scheme.

"Some guys would just want to know that little piece," Guerrieri said, "compared to how everything functions."

The meticulous questioning raised the stakes of the visit among Ohio State's staff. In particular, it required Knowles, who began rebuilding the defense two years ago, to live up to his reputation as a mad scientist.

"I knew we had to be on point," Knowles said. "When you recruit someone like that who understands the game the way he does, it's like a job interview, it's like game day.

"My job is not to be that rah-rah guy and all the beautiful things about Ohio State. My job is to explain the defense in detail, so he understands that I'm going to be able to coach him and make him better on the field with the scheme."

A day after the visit, Caleb Downs called Day, who had left for Mobile, Alabama, to continue visiting with recruits in the South.

Standing in the parking lot of a high school gymnasium, Day learned over FaceTime that Downs would transfer to Ohio State. It prompted him to yell in excitement.

"It was a great feeling," Day said.

Downs' acumen became even more apparent to the staff as he set foot in the Woody Hayes Athletic Center.

When Guerrieri met with him in February to review his plays from 2023, he found Downs could identify each play call. Only the score, time and down and distance overlaid the screen showing the clips of Alabama's games, but Downs recalled coverages and responsibilities.

"It's like a professional golfer who remembers this shot on this hole in this tournament," Guerrieri said.

Teammates took notice as well.

"He's one of the smartest young players I've ever been around," senior linebacker Cody Simon said.

Downs' physical gifts should not be overlooked. He made cameo appearances as a punt returner at Alabama last fall and took one 85 yards for a touchdown in a rout of Chattanooga.

He's talented enough that Day has mused about also featuring him as a running back. Their visit with him in January included proposing ideas about him playing on offense, a level of creativity that heightened Ohio State's appeal.

But the reason that Downs could elevate the Buckeyes' defense, already among the stingiest in the FBS, is owed to the combination of attributes. His legs churn as fast as his mind.

"He's a high-level athlete and you have this brain operating at a click faster," Guerrieri said. "You have both of those things together and you're two steps ahead."

As Downs replaces Josh Proctor as the Buckeyes' "adjuster," the free safety position that gets its nickname due to its responsibilities for making adjustments before the snap, it's never seemed so fitting.

"He's perfect for it," Guerrieri said. ∎

A sure-handed tackler, Caleb Downs takes down Michigan State running back Nate Carter in a 38-7 win over the Spartans. SAMANTHA MADAR/COLUMBUS DISPATCH

August 31, 2024 • Columbus, Ohio

'YOU CAN SEE THE TALENT'

Jeremiah Smith Shines in Debut, Blowout of Akron

By Joey Kaufman

Jeremiah Smith lined up in the slot looking to take off.

It was on second-and-1 near midfield on the opening drive of Ohio State's 52-6 rout of Akron on Saturday. But rather than catch the screen pass from quarterback Will Howard, the ball bounced off his hands, falling incomplete.

"I can't really explain that," Smith said. "I was just mad at my myself."

The moment proved to be a blip in a head-turning debut for Smith, the freshman receiving phenom.

When he returned to the sideline, there was no alarm among the Buckeyes.

"Nobody batted an eye," coach Ryan Day said. "Nobody said a word."

Smith, who was the top-ranked high school prospect in the nation in the last recruiting cycle, had inspired a wealth of confidence since enrolling at Ohio State in January.

"None of us were worried about him at all," Howard said. "It's a drop. It's uncharacteristic."

It was clear Howard trusted Smith as soon as their next possession. On third-and-10 at their 25-yard line, he found Smith on a curl route to move the chains, the first of three connections on a series that was capped by his 16-yard touchdown catch.

Smith reached the end zone with a snag over cornerback Joey Hunter on a fade route.

"He was pressed," Howard said, "so I tried to put it up over the top, and he made a little adjustment and came back to it. That's all I have to do. Just give him a chance, and he's going to do the rest."

His 6-foot-4 frame made him a frequent target for Howard, the former Kansas State quarterback who transferred to Ohio State this year. Smith finished with six receptions for 92 yards and two touchdowns to lead the Buckeyes.

Smith's second touchdown came in the second quarter when he ran a slant over the middle for a 9-yard scoring haul.

He said his favorite grab was his longest one, a 45-yard reception in the third quarter when he got past safety Daymon David and pulled in the pass from Howard with only his left hand.

"We see it every day in practice," Day said. "We knew he was going to settle in."

In front of an announced crowd of 102,011 at Ohio Stadium, Smith seemed unburdened by the weight of expectations many of them had placed upon him.

"I don't really feel pressure," Smith said. "I just want to go out there and play football and win

Freshman wide receiver Jeremiah Smith had a memorable debut with six catches for 92 yards and two touchdowns. ADAM CAIRNS/COLUMBUS DISPATCH

games. I know all the hype around me was crazy coming in. I just wanted to come in and work and not be all about hype, impress my coaches and my peers around me and teammates."

He made an impression on them this weekend, recovering from the shaky first series, which also included being flagged for a false start.

Howard referred to it as a "next-play mentality."

"Mental toughness is the ability to move on to the next most important thing," he said. "We knew his maturity level. He came back and had a great game."

Day, who at times sought to temper expectations for the heralded receiver in preseason camp, was a little less restrained reflecting on the debut.

"Sometimes you look at him," he said, "and you don't think he's quite human, but he is. He's going to make a few early mistakes, but not many. You can see the talent." ■

Opposite: Transfer quarterback Will Howard completed 17 of 28 passes for 228 yards and three touchdowns in his debut with the Buckeyes. ADAM CAIRNS/COLUMBUS DISPATCH

Above: Running back James Peoples had six carries for 30 yards and a touchdown in the comfortable Ohio State win over Akron. ADAM CAIRNS/ COLUMBUS DISPATCH

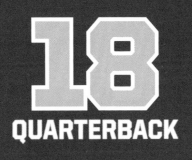

18
QUARTERBACK

WILL HOWARD

How Kansas State Transfer Navigated a Long, Painful Road to Become Ohio State's Quarterback

By Bill Rabinowitz • September 5, 2024

For months, Will Howard wondered what it would feel like.

He had transferred from Kansas State to Ohio State in January 2024 for one last chance at glory.

Howard experienced extreme highs and lows in his four years with the Wildcats, but playing for the Buckeyes is different. The expectations for the 2024 team are immense. An Ohio State quarterback must be oak-tree strong.

At 6-feet-4 and 235 pounds, Howard is sturdy physically. The Downingtown, Pennsylvania, native believes the crucible he has endured has made him mentally strong as well.

For the first time in his college career, Howard knows he is firmly the starting quarterback. It was never really that way at Kansas State. It is a status he relishes, a responsibility he embraces.

Howard passed his first test in the 52-6 victory over Akron. He overcame a slow start to throw for three touchdowns and made some timely runs. Howard looked fully comfortable and in command of a team he joined less than eight months ago.

Bigger tests await. Maybe not against Western Michigan, but certainly at Oregon and at Penn State and in late November against Michigan and then the postseason.

"C.J. (Stroud) said it: Pressure is a privilege," Howard said. "I've experienced pressure at varying levels. But definitely this is the biggest stage and the most amount of pressure that is going to be put on me.

"I know Ohio State fans are hungry. They want to win. We are, too."

Howard knows pressure can work both ways. It can stifle, or it can liberate. He vows to treat it as the latter.

"Go out there and play loose and have fun and play with intensity, and freaking give it all you've got," Howard said, "because that's the only way I know how to do things."

Howard was special from the start

William Thomas Howard is the oldest of Bob and Maureen Howard's four children. Will is named for two of Maureen's brothers, one older and one younger, who died shortly after birth. Will was born on Sept. 24, 2001, two days after Thomas' birthday.

Quarterback Will Howard took a winding journey to Ohio State, but it paid off for him and the Buckeyes in the long run. ADAM CAIRNS/COLUMBUS DISPATCH

"Obviously, that was a difficult time for my parents," Maureen said, "so I told them, 'If it's a boy, it's going to be William Thomas after my brothers.' He's got two special guardian angels for sure."

Will has felt that.

"Whenever I hear my mom or grandma talk about it, it felt like I'm carrying something a little bigger than myself," he said. "I have to carry on their legacy with me. It's pretty cool."

Will was a big kid from the start, typical for a Howard. His younger brother, Ryan, a freshman Kansas State offensive lineman, is 6-7. He has uncles taller than that. Will outgrew his baby swaddle early, causing his mom to create a sleep outfit that eventually became his family's business.

"He was just a pleasure," Maureen said. "He was a happy, adorable, fun, pleasant kid from Day 1. Super smart. Super athletic. He loved balls and sports from Day 1."

The Howards bought a Little Tikes basketball hoop when Will was a toddler. His parents watched stunned as he sank 30 baskets in a row.

"I remember telling Bob's brother, 'That's not normal,'" Maureen said. "His hand-eye coordination was pretty amazing from the beginning."

Howard played above his age in youth sports, which included basketball and baseball. Everything came easy to him athletically. But starting with his sophomore year at Downingtown West High School, every year brought adversity.

His talent was undeniable as a sophomore, but the Whippets had a senior quarterback who had started the previous year. Coach Mike Milano told the quarterbacks and their parents that there would be an open competition and charted every rep throughout the process. Howard won the competition, but feelings were bruised.

"The other kid had all his peers in that senior class," Milano said.

Howard heard scuttlebutt that Downingtown West was sacrificing the season for the future.

"That was a tough year," Howard said. "I can't lie.

"I don't think they had any true animosity toward me as a person. It was more toward the decision and the coaches. That's what I tried to cling to. I don't try to go out there and show them up and be macho. I just went out there and worked."

That won over his teammates.

"He was positive, he was humble, he was honest, he was motivated and he was a leader, even in the 10th grade," Milano said. "It's just who he is."

Howard played well enough to be regarded as a budding star entering his junior year. High-profile programs such as Penn State and several in the Atlantic Coast Conference were recruiting him. Howard led the Whippets to an undefeated record heading into their midseason showdown against rival Coatesville.

"We hate Coatesville," Howard said. "It runs deep in town. We hadn't beaten them since I was in the eighth grade."

In that showdown, Howard got flushed out of the pocket. As he turned to throw, a pass-rusher hit him from behind and pinned Howard's right arm to his chest. Howard tried throwing with his left hand and fell awkwardly. He broke his right wrist, which required surgery to install permanent plates and metal screws.

What Milano remembered most about the injury was how Howard handled it. He said Howard missed practice only on the day he had surgery. Milano moved the tight end to quarterback. Howard became his de facto coach.

"My staff still busts my bones because I made a comment to the newspaper that Will Howard became the best coach on the staff," Milano said. "He just coached his tail off, helping this guy lead us three rounds deep in the playoffs. It's a pretty amazing story."

The injury stalled Howard's recruitment,

which took another hit when he broke his left wrist dunking a basketball in gym class. Colleges that had been courting him backed off.

"I just felt helpless," Howard said. "I couldn't do anything because I've got a broken arm with a plate and screws in it."

Howard sent highlight tapes to different colleges hoping to generate interest. He sent one to Kansas State because he was a fan of Philadelphia Eagles quarterback Carson Wentz, whose North Dakota State coaches had been hired at KSU.

He heard back a couple of hours later. Within days, Kansas State offered a scholarship and an official visit.

Howard thought it unlikely he'd go there because of the distance. Maureen Howard believed it such a long shot she didn't go on that April 2019 trip.

"I thought it was just a shot in the dark, like, 'Hey, I'm taking a trip to a cool Big 12 school,' " he said.

But Howard loved his visit. Two months later, he committed.

Howard had tough start at K-State

Howard enrolled at Kansas State in January 2020. Two days earlier, he played in his last basketball game for Downingtown West, finishing a 1,000-point career.

The Pennsylvania kid suddenly found himself in Manhattan, Kansas, five states and an 18-hour drive away. Homesickness quickly set in.

"I was a mess," he said. "I didn't know if this was the right thing to do. My mom had to come out and see me once or twice."

In March, COVID-19 shut things down just as spring break arrived. At first, Howard welcomed a chance for extra time at home. But players weren't permitted back until June 1 and then had to live alone.

That was tough for Howard, who had already formed a bond with his roommate, offensive lineman Sam Shields, who's from Manhattan and whose family provided a support system.

COVID drastically affected preparation for the season. Howard hadn't taken a single practice rep when training camp began. His goal was to make the 70-man travel roster. Early in camp, he played well enough that winning the backup job behind fifth-year starter Skylar Thompson became realistic.

In KSU's first game, Thompson got injured and coaches inserted Howard. On his first pass, he got hit and sprained the AC joint in his throwing shoulder, an injury about which he and his coaches kept quiet.

Thompson returned for the next game but tore a pectoral muscle the following week and was lost for the season. The job was now Howard's, ready or not.

He played well in a win over Kansas, but then the season collapsed. Kansas State lost its last five games.

The low point might have come against Iowa State, a 45-0 loss. Several players had COVID. Howard was 3 of 9 for 32 yards with an interception.

"We wanted to be the tough guys that played through everything, but we shouldn't have played that game," Howard said.

Howard was miserable. He was living alone because of COVID-forced isolation. His shoulder ached. Every time his mom left after visiting, he got emotional.

"I really struggled that freshman year," Howard said. "It took me a while to get my confidence back from that because I was an 18-, 19-year-old kid that didn't have many reps in college under my belt and probably wasn't ready.

"I look back and I don't know how I did it. There were some plays where I just wanted to get the motion right. I didn't know where the motion was coming from, let alone what the defense is doing."

He struggled on the field, but his teammates noticed how he handled the adversity.

"I remember us other freshmen being like, 'Holy cow, he's really out there leading our offense right now, and I'm struggling to learn the playbook,' " Shields said.

"Obviously, he went through his ups and downs, but I couldn't have more respect for what he went through that season."

Howard's ups and downs continue

Thompson, now a backup with the Miami Dolphins, returned for a final season as a starter in 2021. But he got hurt in the second game against Southern Illinois.

Howard relieved him and admittedly pressed.

"It just couldn't have been a worse scenario," he said. "Everyone loves Skylar. He's been there for six years. He's given his all to the program, and you're just the guy that nobody really wants."

Howard played better the next week against Nevada and the game felt like fun for him for the first time in a long time. Thompson then returned and played until he was hurt again in the next-to-last game of the regular season.

Howard had already played in four games, so if he played the next week against Texas, that would be unable to redshirt. Coach Chris Klieman and Howard's position coach met with Howard and said they wanted him to start.

"They told me, 'We want to gain momentum going into next year, like taking over, this is your team. We're going to let you go out there and do your thing and spin the ball and go play because we have nothing to lose,'" Howard said.

But Howard threw only 13 passes, completing nine for 65 yards, though he ran for 82 yards and a touchdown in the KSU loss. After the game, Klieman fired the offensive coordinator.

Three weeks later, Howard was blindsided when Nebraska quarterback Adrian Martinez announced he would transfer to Kansas State.

"I just felt betrayed," Howard said. "I felt like they lied to me. Do I understand why they did it? Absolutely. I hadn't really proved myself yet. But the fact they told me all those things to make me burn my redshirt, that was frustrating."

Though coaches told Howard that Martinez wouldn't be handed the job, he knew it would take something drastic for that not to happen. The transfer portal was an option, but Howard stayed at Kansas State.

"He was like, 'I'm going to bet on myself and stay here, work as hard as I can and I'm going to get that job,'" said Shields, his roommate.

Martinez started the first six games before injuring a leg in the seventh game against TCU. Howard entered and led the Wildcats on four consecutive touchdown drives, though he later sprained the AC joint in his non-throwing shoulder.

The next week, Martinez was questionable for the Oklahoma State game. Howard said Martinez told coaches right before kickoff that he wasn't ready.

This was Howard's chance and he seized it. He threw for four touchdowns in a 48-0 win. The job was now his. Kansas State won three of its next four games to reach the Big 12 title game, where the Wildcats upset No. 3 TCU in overtime.

Howard ready for a new chapter

Though Kansas State lost to Alabama in the Sugar Bowl, Howard entered 2023 with confidence.

"Coming off that year, I was like, 'OK, I've finally figured it out,'" he said. "I finally got there. I finally made it through that stuff that I had to get through last year. Going into last year, I was like, I'm finally the guy."

But nothing about Howard's Kansas State journey was ever straightforward. The Wildcats signed a dynamic four-star quarterback, Avery Johnson from Wichita. The home-state freshman was the shiny new toy, and Kansas State fans clamored to see him unleashed.

Those demands grew louder when Howard threw three interceptions in a loss to Oklahoma State in early October. Johnson saw extensive playing time the next two games.

"I was like, 'Are you guys kidding me? Are you guys going to do this again?'" Howard said.

He did remain the starter as Kansas State

Will Howard often found a way to rise to the occasion with championship results for the Ohio State Buckeyes. ADAM CAIRNS/COLUMBUS DISPATCH

went 8-4 and set the school career record with 48 touchdown passes.

Howard is grateful for his time as a Wildcat, but by the end of the season, he was ready for the next chapter.

"I have nothing bad to say about my time at K-State," Howard said. "I loved the people. I loved all of the relationships that I had. Overall, there were ups and downs and there were struggles, but I wouldn't trade any of it for the world. I think it made me the person and the player that I am today."

Howard entered the transfer portal in December 2023, but he was not intent on continuing his college career.

"Deep down in my mind, I think I was ready to go to the NFL," he said.

He got a late invitation to the Senior Bowl and a draft projection that he would likely be taken in the fourth round or later.

But he wants to enter the NFL as a higher draft pick to enhance his chances of becoming a starter in the pros, so he had discussions with Miami and USC.

He also talked with Ohio State coach Ryan Day and liked what he heard.

"Once I found out about this opportunity, I was fired up," he said.

But the Buckeyes wanted to wait until the Cotton Bowl, which tested Howard's patience.

"I was eager (to commit)," Howard acknowledged. "I was tired of waiting."

After Ohio State's dispiriting 14-3 loss to Missouri in which quarterback Devin Brown was injured early, the Buckeyes pulled the trigger.

Howard said he told coaches pursuing him in the portal that he sought two things: a chance to win a national championship and a place where he could improve his draft stock.

"There's no place like this when it comes to those two things," he said of Ohio State.

Conversations with OSU players Emeka Egbuka, TreVeyon Henderson and Donovan Jackson also impressed him.

"Not only are they unbelievable players, but they're freaking good people, people I want to play with," Howard said.

Howard 'a true joy to be around'

Howard enrolled in January. He was the favorite to win the job over Brown and freshmen Lincoln Kienholz, Julian Sayin and Air Noland, but Day did not guarantee anything.

Day is notoriously tough on his quarterbacks until they prove themselves worthy. The coach asked Howard how receptive he would be to hard coaching.

"I said, 'Yes, I need it,'" Howard said. "I didn't say, 'Yeah, that's OK.' I said, 'I need you to coach me hard.' I knew I wasn't the player I needed to be."

Howard had to learn a new playbook and get to know his new coaches and teammates. He also needed to lose weight. He weighed 249 when he enrolled, drawing the ire of strength coach Mickey Marotti.

"Coach Mick gave me a hard time about being pretty tubby for a while," he said.

Given everything that was new to him, it wasn't surprising Howard struggled early in spring practice. It wasn't until halfway through that it began to click.

"I was almost pissed at the end of spring because I'm finally feeling comfortable, and now we're done," Howard said.

He spent the next several months watching video with Day and on his own and working with his personal quarterback coach, Jeff Christensen, to refine his fundamentals.

A quarterback must also be a leader, and Howard is a natural one. But he knew he couldn't rush it. He made a point of developing relationships with all his teammates.

"I've said this a million times, but people don't

care how much you know until they know how much you care," Howard said. "If they don't respect someone, they're not going to listen to them.

"I wanted to come in and get to know guys, let them know I'm here for the right reasons, we're all on the same page and that I want to be a part of this with them."

By all accounts, he did that.

"You wouldn't know it was a challenge, just by the way he carries himself," said Egbuka, a senior wide receiver. "He's very professional but also very down to earth.

"He's a very funny guy. He lightens the room when he walks in. He's a true joy to be around. You can throw Will into any setting and he's going to get along with everybody there. He's definitely upped the team chemistry in the locker room."

'I almost have to pinch myself'

When Day announced Aug. 15 that Howard had won the quarterback competition, it was no surprise. Day already seems to have more comfort with Howard than he did with Kyle McCord, last year's starter.

"I think there's a level of trust there," Day said of his relationship with Howard. "He wants to be a great player, and he knows if he buys into this offense, he buys into this team and he buys into our culture that he's going to do that. We've seen all that and more so far."

Howard has lost 15 pounds and re-sculpted his body. He ran 22.1 mph in testing, the fastest of Ohio State's quarterbacks. He believes he is throwing better than ever.

Howard is quick to praise the talent of his Kansas State teammates, but his teammates at Ohio State are at a different level. He knows he is set up for success.

"It's a blessing," he said. "It's kind of surreal that I'm the guy for the Buckeyes. I'm the quarterback for the Buckeyes. A lot of people want to say, 'It's your

team now. How do you feel?'

"But I don't like when people say it's 'my team,' because that takes away from the other guys. I'm just one of 11."

The Buckeyes have not shied away from saying that anything less than a national championship, including a win over Michigan and a Big Ten title, would be a failure.

"If we're not shooting for the 'natty,'" Howard said, "then why are we even out here, especially at a place like this?"

Shields, his Kansas State roommate, has no doubt he can handle it because of his experience as a Wildcat.

"I think he's so calloused," he said. "I think he's got very thick skin now from all he went through, both the highs and the lows."

Howard agrees. He savors this opportunity, to be on an elite team and firmly the starter.

"I almost have to pinch myself out here every day," he said. "I'm playing for Ohio State. I'm potentially on the biggest stage that I could possibly be on. This is all that I dreamed of growing up. I haven't had this much fun playing football in a while." ∎

NO. 2 OHIO STATE 56, WESTERN MICHIGAN 0
September 7, 2024 • Columbus, Ohio

A LONG TIME COMING

OSU Offense Finally Lights Fireworks Early to Thrash Western Michigan

By Rob Oller

The fireworks finally appeared early for Ohio State in the Horseshoe.

Boom ... a magnificent Jeremiah Smith exploding for a 70-yard touchdown in a 56-0 win against Western Michigan.

Bang ... multiple Quinshon Judkins rockets fanning out over the Broncos for 108 yards and a pair of 23-yard touchdowns, with TreVeyon Henderson adding two TDs of his own.

Kapow ... a sparkling Will Howard lighting up the night with his arm, then adding a surprise pop-pop — like one of those delayed action pyrotechnics that fool you — with a TD run.

By the time the show ended, the Buckeyes had three touchdowns in the first quarter — the most first-quarter points since scoring 21 against Indiana in 2022 — and had put up TDs on five of their first six possessions. Wide-eyed adults in Ohio Stadium sat mesmerized like kids on the Fourth of July.

This is what we came to see!

It was spectacular. It was real. And it was a long time coming. The Buckeyes have enough offensive fireworks to make neighborhood dogs howl through the night, but for whatever reason they have struggled to light the fuse in the first quarter, which has annoyed coach Ryan Day to no end. Over the past year, Day resembled a frustrated camper trying to strike a match in the wind.

It all changed against Western Michigan, a decent Mid-American Conference team that gave Wisconsin all it could handle last week before the Badgers pulled away in the fourth quarter.

But Wisconsin is a bottle rocket compared to the powder keg that is Ohio State, and that ammunition dump finally blew, showing what this offense can do when it ignites.

Let's begin with Howard, who inexplicably entered the WMU game with zero buckeye leaf stickers on his helmet. At least that's what several TV viewers texted me during the first quarter, which is the kind of "did you notice...?" question I get when the game's outcome is decided in the first 10 minutes.

Did you notice Brutus looks thinner?

Did you notice Ryan Day's beard looks thicker?

Did you notice Will Howard's helmet has no stickers?

Maybe Connor Stalions noticed, but I didn't, because a) it's hard to count helmet stickers and OSU first downs at the same time, especially when the Buckeyes finished with 30 of the latter to WMU's six; and b) why wouldn't Howard's helmet have any

Running back TreVeyon Henderson did plenty of damage in limited work with 10 carries for 66 yards and two touchdowns. ADAM CAIRNS/COLUMBUS DISPATCH

stickers? True, the Buckeyes slept through the first quarter of last week's win against Akron, but the OSU quarterback had to do enough to earn at least one leaf decal, right?

Normally, I would leave the buckeye leaves investigation to our Ohio State buckeye leaf reporter, but since that person turns out to be me — you learn something new every day — I pursued Stickergate like it was something Jim Harbaugh masterminded.

But by late in the first quarter, when I first focused my binoculars on Howard's helmet, I saw several stickers affixed to the glistening silver shell. *What are these fans and viewers talking about?*

I dug deeper. You're welcome. According to an OSU spokesperson, an equipment person either replaced or reconditioned the shell on Howard's helmet this week and forgot to replace the five buckeye leaf stickers the QB received for the Akron game.

To make a long story longer, the sticker shock was corrected before OSU began its final possession of the first half. So to summarize: Howard's helmet began the day with no buckeye leaves and began the second half with five.

All the above is moot, of course, because after completing 18 of 26 passes for 292 yards and a touchdown, and after scoring on a 6-yard keeper to make it 35-0 before halftime, Howard's helmet undoubtedly will have a dozen leaf stickers stuck to his plastic dome when OSU returns from its upcoming off week. It would have been more, except he missed on a deep ball to Smith that might have gone for six and also was off target on a throw to tight end Jelani Thurman.

"That throw I (missed) to Jeremiah really hurt me for a little bit, but I think I played a pretty clean game for the most part," Howard said. "Coming out

of a game like that, those are the ones that sting, that I don't want to let happen again."

If you are an OSU fan, you have to feel warm and fuzzy after hearing the starting QB nitpick himself in a 56-0 game.

"There were still some plays we left out there, some meat we left on the bone," Howard said, explaining the offense has room to "evolve" into something even better than what it showed against the Broncos.

Maybe, but putting up 683 yards of offense and scoring six rushing touchdowns for the first time since 2019 against Maryland is going to be hard to beat.

Day joined his quarterback in insisting there is room for improvement, and of course there is. But for one night, the fireworks were something to see. Judkins showed an impressive ability to cut to daylight. Smith caught five passes for 119 yards and Emeka Egbuka added five catches for 98. And we haven't even addressed the defense, which earned its first shutout since a 42-0 rout of Cincinnati in 2019.

The defense was expected to dominate. The offense was more of a mystery going in, but struck the match early and boom, the scoreboard lit up. Keep this up and the blowout wins and buckeye stickers will pile up fast. ∎

Jeremiah Smith continued his stellar start to his Ohio State career with five catches for 119 yards and a touchdown in the shutout of Western Michigan. ADAM CAIRNS/COLUMBUS DISPATCH

NO. 3 OHIO STATE 49, MARSHALL 14

September 21, 2024 • Columbus, Ohio

IN CONTROL

Emeka Egbuka Reminds Everyone of His Importance to OSU Offense

By Joey Kaufman

Quarterback Will Howard dumped off a pass to Emeka Egbuka. As Ohio State faced a second-and-8 on its first possession in a 49-14 win over Marshall on Saturday, Egbuka caught the screen and took off. Bolting toward open space near midfield, he went 68 yards to reach the end zone.

"I knew he was gone after he crossed into that third level," Howard said.

Egbuka reflected on his touchdown with a heavy dose of humility.

"It was by no feat of my own that I was able to score," Egbuka said.

The blocks of his teammates on the offensive line and his fellow receivers helped pave the path to the north end of Ohio Stadium. He gave credit to all of them, as well as offensive coordinator Chip Kelly for the play design.

"A toddler could have walked that one in," Egbuka said. "It was wide open."

But Egbuka's burst, the speed that allowed him to separate from the Thundering Herd defenders, was no small thing and offered a reminder to observers of the Buckeyes.

While a lot of offseason attention centered on the high-profile additions to the Buckeyes'

offense such as Mississippi transfer running back Quinshon Judkins and heralded freshman receiver Jeremiah Smith, Egbuka remains a critical weapon for Howard.

In 2022, when Egbuka had a 1,151-yard season, the slot receiver was overshadowed by Marvin Harrison Jr. The next year, Egbuka was hampered by an ankle injury.

But as a senior, a fully healthy Egbuka has reemerged as one of Ohio State's premier playmakers. He finished with five catches for 117 yards and one touchdown against the Thundering Herd.

One of them was on a key 7-yard reception on third-and-4 late in the second quarter that extended a scoring drive. After the Buckeyes picked up the first down, running back TreVeyon Henderson ran for a 14-yard touchdown.

Egbuka's receptions added up to his first 100-yard receiving performance since he had eight catches for 112 yards and a touchdown in a loss to Georgia in a College Football Playoff semifinal two years ago.

He was close to the feat two weeks ago against Western Michigan, finishing with five receptions for 98 yards before accomplishing it Saturday.

"Obviously it's fun to be able to perform at a very high level," Egbuka said, "but I never really tried to

TreVeyon Henderson and the Ohio State rushing attack piled up 280 yards and five touchdowns in the easy win. BARBARA J. PERENIC/COLUMBUS DISPATCH

hang my hat on the statistics. If I had zero catches a day, but I still ran all the right routes and did all the right things, it doesn't make me any less of a player. I could have gone for 300 yards a day, but that's just because the ball came my way.

"So I try to do what I can with the opportunities that I am presented. If the ball comes my way, make the play, and if it doesn't, it's not really something I can control." ■

Above: Tight end Will Kacmarek shared in the fun against Marshall, one of eight Buckeyes with a reception. SAMANTHA MADAR/COLUMBUS DISPATCH.

Opposite: Running back Quinshon Judkins (1) celebrates teammate Will Howard (18) after scoring a touchdown during the second half of the win over Marshall. BARBARA J. PERENIC/ COLUMBUS DISPATCH

NO. 3 OHIO STATE 38, MICHIGAN STATE 7

September 28, 2024 • East Lansing, Michigan

TO THE RESCUE

Smith, Downs Help Pull Ohio State from Choppy Waters

By Rob Oller

When Ohio State was struggling against a nasty rip tide of a road game, Jeremiah Smith and Caleb Downs entered the choppy waters to save the day.

The two Buckeyes — Smith, a freshman wide receiver, and Downs, a sophomore safety — were the best players on the field Saturday night in OSU's 38-7 win against Michigan State. They needed to be, because the No. 3 team in the country looked more like the No. 3 team in the Columbus Central Catholic League. As the offense flailed and the defense failed early against the unranked Spartans, it was just another day at the beach for Smith and Downs, whose outstanding performances have been the constant through a 4-0 start.

Did I mention that Ohio State's struggles came early? Or was that against Marshall? Or Akron? Yes and yes. Oh well, it's not how to start it's how you finish, right? At least until the CFP, which OSU should qualify for. Then how you start matters. A lot.

But we're getting ahead of ourselves. Back to Spartan Stadium. I'm not saying OSU was about to go glug, glug, glug in its first road game of the season — mostly because MSU kept throwing the Buckeyes life preservers in the form of two lost fumbles deep inside OSU territory, a dropped interception and a poor punt that led to an OSU touchdown — but you know how you see that person struggling in the water and aren't sure if they are in serious trouble or clowning around? Then you realize something isn't right. For two quarters, this was that.

Your brain tells you the Buckeyes are too talented to gulp water, but your eyes see what they see — an offense that was out of sync and a defense that was ready to sink. Quarterback Will Howard threw an interception, blaming it on a bad decision, and almost threw another in the end zone, when MSU defender Malik Spencer dropped a ball right in his hands. The run game was just OK. Tailback Quinshon Judkins was ordinary. TreVeyon Henderson a little better than that. Wide receiver Emeka Egbuka, normally sure-handed, dropped two passes. It was that kind of half.

The defense? Not much better. Maybe worse. At least for awhile. The Buckeyes gave up 186 yards the first half before buttoning things up and allowing MSU only 60 yards the second half. Strong.

Clunker games happen. The thing is, if not for two incredible catches by Smith that allowed OSU to take a 24-7 lead into halftime, and without Downs coming up from his safety position to stuff the Spartans when it seemed like no other OSU

Jeremiah Smith battles with Michigan State defensive back Ed Woods in the hard-fought 38-7 victory.
SAMANTHA MADAR/COLUMBUS DISPATCH

defender could, or would, this game likely plays out differently. Again, I'm not saying the Buckeyes would have lost, but it's no sure thing they would have won.

Don't take my word for it. Listen to Ohio State coach Ryan Day.

"(Downs) made a huge difference," Day said. "It was at that turning point where they were moving the ball some and he got us going back there. It felt like it turned the momentum for us on defense.

"Caleb played great tonight. Showed up in a big way in a bunch of different spots. You can just see the acceleration, how fast he plays. Part of that is his athleticism, but the other part is how he prepares."

Downs is a beast, plain and simple. And a smart one. Senior cornerback Jordan Hancock called his teammate a stabilizing force and on-field coach.

"There's a lot of questions I ask him ... so he feels like a coach on the field and that's exactly what we need in our secondary," Hancock said.

Downs tied linebacker Sonny Styles for the team lead in tackles with six, which is not what you want from the safety position, because it means MSU too often reached the second level. But without Downs doing his thing, who knows if the defense would have snapped from its lethargy. He tackles so emphatically that it sends a message to teammates that this is the way the game should be played.

As for Smith, well, good as advertised. His two catches on the late first-half scoring drive that gave OSU a 17-point cushion were as spectacular as it gets, and that's coming from someone who covered some of OSU's best, including David Boston, Santonio Holmes, Michael Jenkins, Michael Thomas and of course Chris Olave, Jaxon Smith-Njigba and Garrett Wilson.

The first catch, thrown by Howard into double coverage down the sideline, saw Smith go up and over the defenders and make a one-handed grab for a 27-yard gain with 50 seconds left. Then, after Devin Brown replaced Howard, who left for one play after getting the wind knocked out of him on a hit, Smith again made a one-handed catch, this time extending his right arm and snatching Brown's pass for a 17-yard touchdown.

Day undoubtedly sleeps better knowing he has Smith always at the rescue.

"Devin stepped up in a big way and came in for Will and delivered that throw, but what an unbelievable catch," Day said. "I can't believe he caught it."

Egbuka could.

"He has all the intangibles that you want in a prototypical receiver," Egbuka said. "He's tall, fast and strong, but just his ability to seek knowledge and want to learn. He doesn't necessarily have to listen to everything I say or coach (Brian Hartline) says, but he takes it in and applies it on the field."

For the Buckeyes' sake, it's good he does. Ditto Downs. They both swing momentum. They save the day. Two football lifeguards ready to rescue. ∎

TreVeyon Henderson made the most of just seven carries, finishing with 69 yards on the ground.
SAMANTHA MADAR/COLUMBUS DISPATCH

NO. 3 OHIO STATE 35, IOWA 7

October 5, 2024 • Columbus, Ohio

'IT'S A LOT OF FUN'

Ohio State Defense Continues Turnover Trend Against Hawkeyes

By Joey Kaufman

When Cade McNamara sidestepped Ohio State defensive tackle Tyleik Williams in the pocket, he ran into Jack Sawyer.

The result was a fumble.

Sawyer, the senior defensive end who is one of the Buckeyes' premier pass rushers, punched the ball loose from McNamara, the veteran Iowa passer, as he seized the opportunity to wreak havoc.

"Quarterbacks have the ball exposed the most," Sawyer said.

Following the strip sack, the ball rolled onto the Ohio Stadium turf, and linebacker Cody Simon jumped on it.

The turnover was a momentum-shifting sequence in Ohio State's 35-7 win over Iowa on Saturday, allowing the Buckeyes to regain possession at the Hawkeyes' 19-yard line and continue a barrage of scoring in the third quarter. They reached the end zone three plays later.

It also continued a trend, marking the third consecutive game in which the Buckeyes forced a fumble.

"It's definitely a point of emphasis for us," Sawyer said.

The Buckeyes made stripping the ball a priority over the offseason. Though they featured one of the best defenses in the nation last fall, they were in the middle of the pack in the Football Bowl Subdivision in forcing fumbles. Among the 14 teams in the Big Ten in 2023, only Michigan State and Wisconsin forced fewer than Ohio State's eight.

Five games into this season, the Buckeyes have forced six fumbles, including another one in the fourth quarter against the Hawkeyes when defensive tackle Ty Hamilton hit McNamara as he attempted a pass.

Safety Lathan Ransom, who forced fumbles in the previous weeks against Marshall and Michigan State, leads Ohio State.

"Any defense will tell you they work on poking the ball out," coach Ryan Day said, "and our guys have done a good job of that."

Hamilton's forced fumble, which was recovered by defensive end Kenyatta Jackson at Iowa's 27-yard line, also set up a score for the Buckeyes. After six straight runs positioned Ohio State near the goal line, quarterback Will Howard found Emeka Egbuka for a 3-yard touchdown.

The Buckeyes scored 21 points off turnovers in their latest win, including an interception by cornerback Davison Igbinosun in the third quarter.

"It's a lot of fun," Sawyer said. "When you're playing like that, creating turnovers, getting off the field with big plays, it sparks the offense, it helps us and it gets us fired up." ∎

Freshman sensation Jeremiah Smith hauls in a touchdown with one hand, one of his four catches for 89 yards. SAMANTHA MADAR/COLUMBUS DISPATCH

Safety Sonny Styles tackles Iowa Hawkeyes running back
Kaleb Johnson during the second half of Ohio State's 35-7 win.
ADAM CAIRNS/COLUMBUS DISPATCH

NO. 3 OREGON 32, NO. 2 OHIO STATE 31

October 12, 2024 • Eugene, Oregon

COULDA NOT SHOULDA

Ohio State Had Opportunities to Beat Oregon But Didn't Deserve the Win

By Rob Oller

Ohio State left Oregon wine country spitting sour grapes. It wasn't vintage whine, to be sure.

The Buckeyes tried not to blame anyone but themselves for losing 32-31 to the Ducks. But a great game, and this was that, deserves to be characterized as a classic, not a coulda, shoulda.

Could Ohio State have won in an incredibly loud and energized Autzen Stadium? That's like asking if pigs can fly. Sure, if you pile them into an airplane. Sure, the No. 2 Buckeyes coulda won. But shoulda? No way.

Oregon was better. Period. Ohio State was worse. Period. Oregon (6-0, 3-0 Big Ten) completed passes *down the field* — four of 32 yards or more. The Buckeyes (5-1, 2-1) did not, which is a recurring theme for which no one seems to have the answer. At least not the guys getting handsomely paid. Or maybe they know the answer and that's the problem. How do you say your starting quarterback struggles with the deep ball without throwing him under the bus?

Chip Kelly was careful not to. The Buckeyes' QB coach/offensive coordinator explained that Oregon's defense took away the deep outside of the field, leaving Will Howard no choice but to mostly abandon the deep sideline passes.

"At least that's what it seemed like," Kelly said, not sounding as positive as you would like him to. "If they're going to do that, then you have to take what they're giving us inside."

Ohio State took some successful shots down the middle of the field, including a 25-yard catch by tight end Gee Scott Jr., but when you have Emeka Egbuka and Jeremiah Smith at your disposal, you are wasting their talent by not throwing more deep balls and letting them make plays.

Of course, sometimes those plays go haywire, which brings us to another supposed shoulda. No matter what they say, the Buckeyes should not have been looking at a potential winning 37-yard-or-less field goal in the game's final seconds, because Smith absolutely pushed off Oregon cornerback Nikko Reed on a 7-yard catch to draw a deserved 15-yard offensive pass interference penalty that moved OSU out of field goal range.

From there, the Buckeyes faced second-and-25, then third-and-25 with six seconds left. Howard scrambled for 12 yards, sliding to a stop after the clock reached 0:00. Game over.

"I don't think they necessarily beat us. I think we beat ourselves a little bit," Howard said.

Coach Ryan Day (right) and offensive coordinator Chip Kelly watch warmups before the big game with Oregon. Kelly was the head coach for the Ducks from 2009-12. ADAM CAIRNS/COLUMBUS DISPATCH

Oregon made more big plays than Buckeyes

Sorry, but Oregon beat the Buckeyes. Necessarily.

A trustworthy saying: When a coach or player mentions more than once that "the game did not come down to one play," it usually means that the coach or player thinks the game pretty much came down to one play. In this case, Smith's penalty.

"The one play there, the DB is grabbing on Jeremiah, and Jeremiah is fighting there and they called a flag. That cost us," Day said. "But it shouldn't come down to one play."

No, it shouldn't. And it didn't. It came down to Oregon executing deep passes against the Buckeyes' suddenly hapless secondary, and Ducks quarterback Dillon Gabriel making big throws and a big TD run against a Jim Knowles' defense that once again failed to close the deal. And Day was none too happy about it.

"Overall, just too many explosive plays on the defensive side," Day said, choosing not to single out any individuals. He didn't have to. It was obvious to all that cornerback Denzel Burke was way off his game. The senior struggled both in coverage, getting beat badly on completions of 69 and 48 yards, and with his tackling. He wasn't the only weak spot on a defense that allowed 341 yards passing, failed to contain Ducks tailback Jordan James (115 yards) and registered no sacks, but he was ground zero.

Ohio State suffered from lack of prior competition

It appeared that Ohio State's secondary was shell-shocked by Oregon's offensive talent, which makes sense. The Buckeyes' previous five opponents failed to match up against OSU's superior talent. Not so the Ducks.

"It's my job to create that in practice," Knowles said. "We've got to find a way to ramp up that competition and simulate those situations in a better way."

Indeed.

And yet despite a porous pass defense, a lost fumble and an onside kick that Oregon recovered when the line drive kick bounced off Caleb Downs, Ohio State still had one last chance to go down and score at the end.

"We didn't finish," Day said. "We talk about leaving no doubt and not coming down to one play, and that was this game. So, we can sit here and look at one play here and one play there and complain about a call, but we're not going to do that."

Good, because doing so would suggest the better team lost. It didn't. The better team won. And the other team has work to do. ■

Buckeyes linebacker Cody Simon pressures Oregon Ducks quarterback Dillon Gabriel during the first half. Simon had 10 tackles, but it wasn't enough in the road loss. ADAM CAIRNS/COLUMBUS DISPATCH

Ohio State Season is Far from Over, but Problems Must Be Fixed

By Bill Rabinowitz

An Ohio State team that looked almost flawless through five games against overmatched opponents got smacked by reality.

No. 3 Oregon's 32-31 victory over the No. 2 Buckeyes at Autzen Stadium does not doom Ohio State in a season it has embraced as national championship or bust. The new 12-team College Football Playoff gives the Buckeyes a margin for error.

But the Buckeyes made the kind of errors against the Ducks that must be fixed if they are to make a run for a title.

Quinshon Judkins fumbled at the OSU 28 in the first quarter when it looked like the Buckeyes (5-1) were poised to take control and quiet the raucous crowd after driving 75 yards for a game-opening touchdown.

A face-mask penalty on OSU cornerback Jordan Hancock on a Ducks touchdown allowed them to kick off from the 50. Oregon (6-0) sent a line-drive kick right at Caleb Downs that the safety couldn't handle, and the Ducks recovered. Oregon then kicked a field goal for its first lead.

Such mistakes could be written off as flukes. The inability of the Buckeyes' defense to stop Oregon cannot.

This was an OSU defense that was allowing fewer points and yards than any team in the country. But Akron, Western Michigan, Marshall, Michigan State and Iowa proved to be little preparation for Oregon.

The Buckeyes were almost powerless to stop the Ducks. Oregon gained 496 yards, 300 more than Ohio State's average.

They couldn't stop Oregon on the ground. Jordan James ran 23 times for 115 yards. Quarterback Dillon Gabriel faked almost the entire defense on a 27-yard touchdown run that gave Oregon a 29-28 lead early in the fourth quarter.

But it was Ohio State's failure against Oregon's passing game that was the real eye-opener. Cornerback Denzel Burke said during the week that he looked forward to playing Oregon's speedy receivers.

But Burke, who coined the "natty or bust" mantra in the spring, had a nightmare of a game. In the second quarter alone, Burke was beaten by Evan Stewart on a 69-yard gain and a 10-yard touchdown and by Tez Johnson on a 48-yard touchdown.

Burke was the most obvious culprit, but this was a total unit collapse. The Buckeyes did not sack Gabriel. They did not force a turnover.

"They did their job and we didn't," Ohio State linebacker Cody Simon said. "That's what's going to happen when you don't execute the way you're supposed to.

"We had to get more stops on defense. We needed to help our offense out. They did more than enough to win this game."

In some ways, that's accurate. The Buckeyes gained 467 yards, starting with a flawless opening touchdown drive (though a 32-yard Will Kacmarek catch could have been ruled an Oregon interception). Will Howard completed 28 of 35 passes for 326 yards and three touchdowns. TreVeyon Henderson had a 53-yard run to set up a score.

But offensive coordinator Chip Kelly said the offense was "a little disjointed."

After running for 99 yards in the first quarter, the Buckeyes gained only 42 yards on the ground the rest of the game. It didn't help that left tackle Josh Simmons, arguably the Buckeye who improved most over the offseason, was injured in the second quarter. Day said it appeared Simmons could be lost for the season, a huge blow.

Oregon was intent on taking away Ohio State's deep passing game and mostly did. Howard mostly settled for short- and intermediate-range passes. That worked plenty of the time. Emeka Egbuka (10 catches for 93 yards) made several clutch plays to keep drives alive.

In what seemed like a quiet game, Smith had nine catches for 100 yards. The freshman will undoubtedly remember his offensive pass interference penalty most. It came on the final OSU drive and negated a 9-yard reception to the Oregon 19, pushing the ball back to the 43 instead. (Despite coach Ryan Day's claim that the Oregon defender was grabbing Smith, the receiver clearly pushed off to gain separation.)

This knocked the Buckeyes out of field-goal range, and they never got back inside it. Howard said he thought he'd slid on his 12-yard scramble to the 26 on the final play before time expired, but he was one second too late.

"It sucks," Howard said. "A play like that, you don't want to lose a game like that."

It was the second time in four seasons that Oregon has exposed Ohio State's flaws. In the Ducks' 35-28 victory in Columbus in 2021, the defense's problems were so obvious that Day demoted defensive coordinator Kerry Coombs.

Day is not going to do anything like that this time with Jim Knowles, but the performance at Eugene was a sobering one.

"We've got to look at it all," Day said. "Something we preach a lot is (limiting explosive) plays and keeping it in front, making them work the ball down the field. It didn't happen in this game. So it starts with coaching. We've got to coach it better, demand it better and then drill it better in practice."

The Buckeyes will have ample time for practice. They are off this week before starting the second half of their regular season.

A tough game in early November at No. 4 Penn State awaits, as does, of course, the Michigan game after Thanksgiving. The Buckeyes spoke of a potential rematch with Oregon in the Big Ten championship game. That likely will happen if they take care of business.

"We can sit here and look at one play here, one play there, complain about a call," Day said. "But we're not going to do that. We're going to own it. We're going to get it fixed."

But this night showed that if they don't, Ohio State's season will end in disappointment yet again. Given the expectations for this team, that would be devastating. ■

NO. 4 OHIO STATE 21, NEBRASKA 17

October 26, 2024 • Columbus, Ohio

'NOT CLOSE TO GOOD ENOUGH'

Close Call Against Nebraska Demands Q&A to Sort Out Running Game Woes

By Rob Oller

You probably have questions after the cash-rich Jeff Bezos of college football eked out a 21-17 win against minimum wage Nebraska Saturday in the Shoe — a close call that threatened to end Ohio State coach Ryan Day's 43-game winning streak against unranked teams.

I have questions, too. Fortunately, I also have answers.

I'm calling this segment of the show "Someone has some 'splainin to do."

Let's get to it.

Question: What is wrong with Ohio State's offense?

Answer: Can't run the ball.

Question: How can that be?

Answer: Subpar recruiting, suspect development and a failure to make enough impact in the transfer portal to provide adequate next-man-up depth. Add one key injury to left tackle Josh Simmons and voila (French for "It's a good thing OSU has a passing game.")

Question: If you are tailbacks TreVeyon Henderson and Quinshon Judkins, and you have NFL talent but are running behind a Sun Belt Conference line, what are you thinking?"

Answer (diplomatic version:) "Not being too high, being too low in those situations," Judkins said, explaining his emotions in the wake of watching the run game crawl. "Just believe in my teammates. I know those guys will go out there and execute."

Maybe someday that will be true, but the numbers against the Cornhuskers made that day feel a long way off. Judkins carried 10 times for 29 yards; Henderson was 10 for 25. Quarterback Will Howard made some late drive-extending plays with his legs, but still finished with only 14 yards on eight carries. Overall, OSU gained 64 yards for a 2.1 average, the lowest since stumbling to 62 last season against Maryland. It was only the third time since 2017 that the Buckeyes failed to crack 65 yards on the ground.

Answer (no spin version): Judkins could have taken the handoff, immediately fallen forward and gained almost as many yards per carry as he did slogging behind a line that allowed seven tackles for loss, including two sacks. This is a guy who gained 2,725 yards at Mississippi the past two seasons before transferring to OSU, a guy who was named Southeastern Conference freshman of the year in 2022.

So when Judkins says, "For our offensive line, it wasn't our best day," that is a polite way of saying there was nowhere to go with the ball. He and

Will Howard made the most of his limited throws against Nebraska, completing 13 of 16 passes for 221 yards, three touchdowns and one interception. KYLE ROBERTSON/COLUMBUS DISPATCH

Henderson may not be miserable at the moment, but they cannot be thrilled.

Question: What did Day have to say about the running game?

Answer: You know when you screwed up as a kid and your father would say, "I'm disappointed in you?" Well, this felt like that.

"We didn't run the football," Day said, clearly unhappy with the result. "We only ran for 64 yards. … That's not close to good enough. Under three yards a carry with Quinshon and TreVeyon, that's not getting it done."

Question: What happened? Specifics, please.

Answer No. 1: Let's be honest, this O-line has seldom been great this season. The high point came against Marshall, when the Buckeyes rushed for 280 yards two weeks after gaining 273 against Western Michigan. The most impressive performance (203 yards) came against a tough Iowa defense, but OSU failed to break the 200-yard barrier against Akron (170), Michigan State (185) and Oregon (141).

Given that we're looking at a relatively low bar to begin with — the line was going to be the weak spot in this offense from the get-go — it comes as no surprise that the run game too often is stuck in neutral.

Answer No. 2: Nebraska's defense is not exactly the 1985 Chicago Bears. Last week against Indiana, the Cornhuskers allowed 215 rushing yards, with the Hoosiers averaging 6.5 yards a carry. Something had to have happened for the Buckeyes to buckle this badly up front. And that something was fourth-year tackle Zen Michalski, who struggled mightily filling in for Simmons. Michalski gave up one sack, got away with a hold that looked like he was trying to rope a calf instead of block a defender, and generally looked lost in his first start.

Day was gracious toward Michalski's performance, explaining that nerves may have contributed to the messiness. Also, the tackle was helped off the field after an injury in the fourth quarter. No reason to kick a man when he's down. But Ohio State needs to figure out something with the left side of the line fast — the right side is no great shakes, either, but the left side is more of an emergency situation — or next week's game at Penn State will not end well.

Question: What is the solution?

Answer: That is the $64,000 question or whatever it is linemen make in NIL money these days. Left guard Donovan Jackson moved to left tackle when Michalski went down, with Luke Montgomery taking over at left guard. I'm not sure that's an acceptable long-term fix. Moving Donovan, OSU's best lineman, to another position runs counter to common sense, but what other choice is there? The Buckeyes already have mixed and matched linemen through spring and fall practice trying to find the right combination. It likely has reached the point of having to just coach them up and hope for the best.

Question: Is their best good enough?

Answer: I don't know. And if you're an Ohio State fan that is the scariest response of all. ∎

Wide receiver Carnell Tate hauled in four catches for 102 yards and a touchdown in the close win against Nebraska. KYLE ROBERTSON/COLUMBUS DISPATCH

NO. 4 OHIO STATE 20, NO. 3 PENN STATE 13

November 2, 2024 • State College, Pennsylvania

BACK ON TRACK

Goal-Line Stand, Running Out the Clock Prove OSU's Mettle

By Bill Rabinowitz

Saturday's game was an unquestioned pivot point for No. 4 Ohio State's season.

A loss to Oregon and a shaky performance against Nebraska last week left the Buckeyes with an increasing number of skeptics.

A showdown with No. 3 in front of a record crowd of 111,030 at Beaver Stadium would prove to be a test of Ohio State's mettle.

An early 10-0 deficit added weight to the challenge, but the Buckeyes proved up to it in a 20-13 victory.

"I think it's fair to say we were at a crossroads," coach Ryan Day said. "This was a big game for us. We didn't really want to publicly say that, but we said that behind closed doors."

The win keeps Ohio State's Big Ten title hopes alive and puts them in commanding position for a spot in the 12-team College Football Playoff.

A loss would have all but ended conference championship hopes and given OSU (7-1, 4-1 Big Ten) little margin for error for the playoff. It also would have given ammunition to those critical of Day's performance in the biggest games. Ohio State was 2-6 in games against teams ranked in the top 5 of the Associated Press poll.

Instead, the Buckeyes opened November with a crucial win.

After falling behind early, Ohio State answered with touchdown drives of 74 and 81 yards to take a 14-10 halftime lead. Jayden Fielding kicked two field goals to give OSU a 20-13 lead early in the fourth quarter.

Ohio State's defense then made a goal-line stand with just over five minutes left.

Penn State (7-1, 4-1) had first-and-goal at the 3. Three run plays up the middle got it to the 1. On fourth down, quarterback Drew Allar threw incomplete into a sea of defenders.

The Buckeyes then stayed exclusively on the ground to get four first downs that ran out the clock.

"I said to the team there are no great accomplishments that happen without going through adversity," Day said. "You don't just walk into a season and think you're going to reach your goals. You get backed up against the wall, and you've got to respond."

Howard's homecoming starts shaky but ends triumphantly

OSU quarterback Will Howard, a Downingtown, Pennsylvania, native, dreamed of playing for his home-state school and remains "salty" that Penn State didn't extend an offer.

Defensive back Davison Igbinosun breaks up a pass in the close win over Penn State.
ADAM CAIRNS/COLUMBUS DISPATCH

His performance wasn't exactly the stuff of childhood dreams, certainly at the start. On his first pass, a throw intended for Jeremiah Smith was intercepted by cornerback Zion Tracy and returned 31 yards for a touchdown.

With OSU at the Penn State 13-yard line trying to pad its 14-10 lead in the second quarter, Howard ran for an apparent touchdown. But the call was ruled a touchback on review after it was determined that safety Zakee Wheatley had knocked the ball through the end zone before Howard reached the goal line.

Howard had his moments. He threw two touchdown passes on creative play designs by offensive coordinator Chip Kelly — a 25-yarder to Emeka Egbuka and a 21-yarder to Brandon Inniss in the first half to give Ohio State the halftime lead.

Howard didn't run for a lot of yards, but he was effective on sneaks and then converted third downs with runs that clinched the win on the final drive.

"There's no feeling like it," Howard said. "It wasn't pretty. I probably played my worst game of the year, but man, we willed that game. We talked about it early in the week. We're going to have to will ourselves to win this game, like there's no way we're going to lose. That was the way we played."

Ohio State's defense rises up

The goal-line stand was the highlight of a defense that sometimes bent but didn't yield a touchdown. Penn State drove 61 yards for a field goal on its first possession, but its offense didn't score again the rest of the half. Cornerback Davison Igbinosun, who was called for pass interference three times last week, had two key plays. He broke up a pass for a three-and-out in the first quarter and then made a terrific interception at the end of the second quarter when

he wrested the ball from Harrison Wallace in the end zone. On the previous play, Wallace beat Igbinosun for a 21-yard catch to the 3.

In the second half, the Buckeyes allowed a field goal late in the third quarter that allowed Penn State to cut its deficit to 17-13. OSU shut the door after that.

OSU's run game proves clutch

Day said that getting the running game untracked after rushing for only 64 yards against Nebraska was a priority. With left tackle Josh Simmons out for the season and Zen Michalski also injured, Donovan Jackson moved outside from left guard. Carson Hinzman played left guard.

Jackson gave up two sacks to speedy edge rusher Abdul Carter, but the line performed better overall than it did last week.

When it mattered most, it came through. After the defense's final goal-line stand, the Buckeyes went 58 yards in 11 plays to run out the clock.

"All of our goals are in front of us now," Day said. "We've been through a lot, and now we have to continue to build as we head into the back half of the season. But I can tell you coming out of that locker room, there are a lot of guys that are excited. It's probably the most animated locker room I've been in in a long time." ∎

Linebacker Cody Simon relishes Ohio State's dramatic victory over the Nittany Lions on the road.
ADAM CAIRNS/COLUMBUS DISPATCH

Ryan Day Gets Monkey Off His Back – at Least for Now – at Penn State

By Rob Oller

Ryan Day smiled the kind of knowing smile a coach smiles when he wants to speak in more detail but knows now is not the time.

The past three seasons have been professionally challenging for Day, not because the Ohio State coach struggled to win — he is 39-7 (.848) since 2021 — but because he struggled to win enough against the best teams. And also against teams, think Michigan, that weren't always the best but burnt down the social media message boards if you lost to them.

Day is the next John Cooper, they say.

Fire Day and bring in Mike Vrabel, they say. Or see if Urban is tired of talking into a microphone.

Day is not tough enough.

Day is not this. Day is not that.

Blah, blah, blah.

Yes, Day hears the criticism

Day has heard it all, even if most of the time he acts as if he hasn't heard any of it. A coach who admits he pays attention to "the noise" is an honest coach who honestly probably should not admit it, because to show vulnerability is to risk further insult.

Day whines too much, they say.

But Day tossed risk onto the manure pile at Penn State. (I reference manure only because at one point during Ohio State's 20-13 win in suddenly Unhappy Valley, a breeze blew directly from the nearby animal barns into Beaver Stadium. Or maybe that was the Nittany Lions' goal-line play calling?)

"There's a lot there to unpack that I'm not going to get into all of it," Day said in the small shed PSU uses for a postgame interview room.

Then he kind of got into it.

"But yeah, there's a lot that goes with being the head coach of Ohio State," Day continued, smiling the I-think-you-know-what-I-mean smile. "You can say, 'Ignore everything that goes on,' but your players read it, your coaches read it, your staff members read it, your family reads it, and you have to stay strong in those moments."

Some will point to Day's comments as proof he lacks the killer instinct necessary to beat the best, pointing to the sixth-year coach's 2-6 record against teams ranked in the top-five of the Associated Press poll at the time the games were played.

Now 3-6, by the way.

Day competes more 'than anyone'

Day, a softie? Rubbish, I say. That's like saying the Buckeyes are not tough enough because they wear Jesus Won T-shirts. That kind of old-school thinking needs to be deep-sixed as soon as possible.

But don't take my word for it that Day can become a bit demented about winning. Listen to offensive lineman Donovan Jackson.

"Coach Day wants this more than anybody," Jackson said. "All the stuff he gets put through, he's more of a competitor than anyone on this team."

Day's cup of competitiveness runneth over as the game clock ticked toward 0:00. When the No. 4 Buckeyes sealed the win against No. 3 Penn State with a first down on a Will Howard quarterback keeper with just under one minute to play, Day practically threw his arm out of socket signaling first down. It felt like adrenaline unleashed. Ohio State *finally* put a game away on its last offensive series, and Day's reaction was a culmination of that achievement after seeing the defense *finally* make a huge stop against a top-five team with the game on the line.

For those scoring at home, the previous paragraph contains two finallys. See No. 3 Clemson in 2019. See No. 1 Georgia in 2022. See No. 3 Michigan last season. See No. 3 Oregon three weeks ago. Yes, it's been a long time coming.

"The entire team, the families, they all believe," Day said. "So to go do that, and accomplish what we did today, this game (against) a top five, it feels good. We still have a lot of football ahead of us, but I'm proud of our team."

Buckeyes closed the deal

As he should be. Ohio State did not play flawlessly. At times far from it. When Will Howard threw a pick-six on his opening series, then later fumbled the ball back to Penn State on what looked to be a sure touchdown, well, if you weren't thinking, "Here we go again," then you haven't been paying attention.

But even as Howard's mistakes appeared to portend Ohio State's fate, the Pennsylvania-born QB insisted that despite OSU's struggling Will, the Buckeyes would find a way.

"I probably played my worst game of the year," Howard said, before adding that the discussion all week had been how the Buckeyes would need to will their way to a win, knowing the game would come down to the fourth quarter.

And will it they did, with help from some head-scratching play calling by PSU. Facing first-and-goal from the OSU 3-yard line, the Nits ran three straight plays up the gut for a net of 2 yards before attempting a pass on fourth down.

Quarterback Drew Allar tried to squeeze a pass into tight end Khalil Dinkins in the end zone. Ohio State safety Caleb Downs was having none of it. The Buckeyes' best player broke up the pass, and from there, offensive coordinator Chip Kelly called 10 consecutive runs as OSU smashed its way from the 1-yard line to the Penn State 40 before Howard took a knee to end the game.

And just like that, Ohio State exorcized two demons over a five-minute span. The big-game bugaboos of the past — late-game defensive lapses and offensive inefficiency in the final minutes — were vanquished. At least for one day.

And for one Day, too. ■

NO. 3 OHIO STATE 45, PURDUE 0
November 9, 2024 • Columbus, Ohio

'I'M JUST HAVING FUN'

Jeremiah Smith Breaks Cris Carter's Ohio State Touchdown Record

By Joey Kaufman

Jeremiah Smith said he realized he had broken Cris Carter's four-decades-old record only after he caught a glimpse of the Ohio Stadium video board.

It was late in the second quarter of Ohio State's 45-0 win over Purdue on Saturday when the screen recognized Smith for breaking the mark for receiving touchdowns by a true freshman.

His 17-yard touchdown grab with 27 seconds left until halftime marked his ninth such score.

"I wasn't even thinking about it," Smith said. "That's how crazy it was."

Smith, who had previously broken Carter's true freshman records for receptions and receiving yards, had the chance to further etch his name in the school's record books as soon as he began a drag route.

"They were in man coverage," Smith said, "so I knew the ball was coming to me."

Nyland Green, the Boilermakers' cornerback who was lined up across from Smith, lost ground as the freshman phenom ran over the middle of the field.

Once Smith pulled in the pass from quarterback Will Howard at the 15-yard line, he took off toward the end zone.

While the record was not at the forefront of Smith's mind when he crossed the goal line against Purdue, it was not an afterthought.

It was among the goals he listed for himself in 2024 after he enrolled at Ohio State in January, a snapshot of an intense drive that has allowed him to live up to the lofty expectations that trailed him as the top high school recruit in the nation last year.

But he said he had not dwelled on it much as the season progressed.

"We have so much stuff going on," he said. "So many new plays to go over, so didn't have it on my mind."

Asked whether he had plans to celebrate the milestone, he kept it in perspective.

"It's just a blessing to be able to break the record," Smith said, "but I don't think it's anything to celebrate. I'm just having fun."

So did his teammates.

"Nobody was really shocked," Howard said. "Everyone was like, 'Oh yeah, J.J. is doing his thing again.'"

With 45 receptions for 765 yards and nine touchdowns with three games left in the regular season, Smith figures to add to his totals.

But he said his remaining goals are not

Freshman receiver Jeremiah Smith continued his record-breaking year for Ohio State with six catches for 87 yards and a touchdown in the easy win over Purdue. BARBARA J. PERENIC/COLUMBUS DISPATCH

personal ones. He hopes to help Ohio State (8-1, 5-1) win the Big Ten and College Football Playoff at the end of the year.

The Buckeyes will continue to benefit from having the 6-foot-3 pass catcher as one of the focal points of their passing game.

"As a freshman, I think he's the best receiver in the country," Howard said. "I think we have the three best receivers in the country. I'm lucky to have guys like that doing what they're doing.

"I knew Jeremiah was going to be special from the first time I met him. He's just continued to get better and better. He's a great kid. I'm really happy for him getting that record." ■

Above: Tight end Gee Scott Jr. (88) and Will Howard (18) celebrate during the big win over Purdue. SAMANTHA MADAR/COLUMBUS DISPATCH

Opposite: Receiver Emeka Egbuka finds his way to end zone in the blowout. SAMANTHA MADAR/ COLUMBUS DISPATCH

NO. 2 OHIO STATE 31, NORTHWESTERN 7
November 16, 2024 • Chicago, Illinois

A BITTERSWEET DAY AT THE BALLPARK

Carnell Tate Catches Two Touchdowns in Emotional Chicago Homecoming

By Joey Kaufman

Carnell Tate spent most of his childhood in this city, but he never saw a game at Wrigley Field.

"I don't really watch baseball," Tate said.

Tate had only been to Guaranteed Rate Field, the home of the Chicago White Sox on the South Side.

Any allegiance to one of Chicago's Major League Baseball teams had drifted up the Lake Michigan shoreline by Saturday afternoon.

"I'm a Cubs fan today," Tate grinned.

The club's historic ballpark on the North Side was the scene of an emotional homecoming for Tate.

At least 30 family and friends sat in the stands as he caught four passes for 52 yards and two touchdowns in Ohio State's 31-7 win over Northwestern.

"It was definitely a high emotion," Tate said, "being able to see all the smiles on my family's faces."

Three of them were his sister, father and grandmother.

"Those three mean the most to me," Tate said.

But his return also figured to be bittersweet.

The crowd did not include his mother, Ashley Griggs, who was killed last year in a drive-by shooting only eight miles from the park.

"It's been a lot of ups and downs over the last year," Tate said.

Tate said he leaned on family, as well as Brandon Inniss, his roommate and a fellow sophomore receiver, for support. The two have been close friends for years, having played together on a 7-on-7 team in South Florida.

Tate left Chicago in 2021 as he transferred to the IMG Academy in Bradenton, Florida.

Because of the move, this was the first time many in his family had seen him play a game in person since he was a freshman at Marist High School. The wait added to their anticipation.

"They expected a lot coming back home," Tate said. "They wanted me to put on a show and stuff like that. I just had to wait and see if the ball found my way."

It did on the Buckeyes' first possession when quarterback Will Howard found him for a gain of 5 yards, a completion that put them in a situation to successfully go for it on fourth down.

With friends and family in the stands, Chicago native Carnell Tate had four catches for 52 yards and two touchdowns. ADAM CAIRNS/COLUMBUS DISPATCH

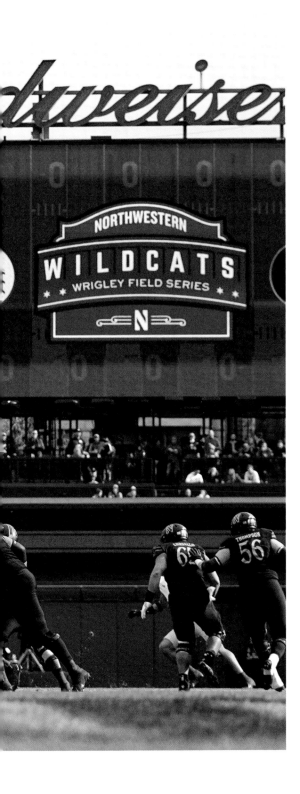

But Tate made his biggest splash later in the second quarter. With 53 seconds left until halftime, Howard floated a pass to him down the sideline. Approaching the end zone on the east side of the park, Tate laid out for a diving catch that resulted in a 25-yard touchdown, padding their lead over the Wildcats.

"I had to go and make a play," Tate said. "Will put the ball out for me to go get."

While Tate anticipated Howard would target him before scoring his first touchdown, his 8-yard touchdown reception in the third quarter was more unexpected. Howard's first look was to Emeka Egbuka out of the slot. But when Egbuka drew two defenders, it left Tate open underneath.

"When the ball's in your hands," Tate said, "you got to make the best of your opportunity."

It was the first time Tate had caught multiple touchdowns in a game in two seasons at Ohio State. In nine games in 2024, he had caught 31 passes for 457 yards and four touchdowns, rounding out the starting trio of Egbuka and star freshman Jeremiah Smith.

Reflecting on Tate's emergence, Buckeyes coach Ryan Day described the wide receiver as a reserved teenager.

Carrying the tragic loss of his mother for the last 15 months, Tate has often kept his emotions private.

"He does not show that every day," Day said.

But his performance provided an opportunity for the rest of the Buckeyes to show their respect for his resolve.

"We say it all the time that the game doesn't care about what you've been through," Day said, "but we do. His teammates do. His coaches do. The people who know Carnell care a lot about him. The way he's handled himself is an example to everybody."

Their admiration only grew over the weekend.

"For him to have the game he had in his home city and stadium," Howard said, "I couldn't be happier for him." ∎

The Wrigley Field stands were packed with Buckeyes fans as they took on the Northwestern Wildcats in Chicago. ADAM CAIRNS/COLUMBUS DISPATCH

NO. 2 OHIO STATE 38, NO. 5 INDIANA 15

November 23, 2024 • Columbus, Ohio

THE STAGE IS SET

A Solid Win Over IU, but is OSU Good Enough to Beat UM, Win it All?

By Rob Oller

The question looms over Buckeye Nation like the massive horseshoe-shaped structure that is impossible to ignore. Just as Ohio Stadium rises 166 feet above the horizon, a constant reminder of the biggest game in town, so the query is ever-present.

Is Ohio State good enough to beat Michigan?

On the surface, the answer seems obvious. Michigan has no quarterback. The Wolverines also have no Connor Stalions. *Of course* the Buckeyes will end that nasty three-game losing streak. Of course.

Are you drinking that poison? After what No. 2 Ohio State did to No. 5 Indiana on Saturday in the Shoe, it might be tempting for OSU fans to take a swig of the dangerous potion. Or even to guzzle enough to believe the Buckeyes are good enough to win the College Football Playoff championship.

Are the Buckeyes up to the task? I think so. But beware. Thinking is not knowing. And no one knows. Not Vegas. Not Lee Corso. Not even AI.

Still, if the 38-15 win against IU is any indication, Ohio State fans should feel good about their chances against Michigan. Or anyone else. I've seen Texas. Good, not great. Ditto Notre Dame, Georgia and Miami (Florida), Penn State? Pulleez. Oregon is legit, but only one point better than Ohio State, and that 32-31 win was in Eugene.

Indiana, with 10 wins for the first time in school history, supposedly was seated at the same table with those brand-name programs, but I never quite believed the Hoosiers hype. What's that line about water returning to its own level? Not to suggest IU was a fraud, but there was some sleight of hand going on.

But magic isn't supposed to be analyzed too closely, lest the mystery gives way to cynicism. So let's give IU its due and agree the Hoosiers (10-1, 7-1) were worthy of something just inside a top-10 ranking. After all, their 34-point average margin of victory against Michigan State, Northwestern and Nebraska is better than OSU's 20-point margin against those common opponents.

And yet the Hoosiers lost by 23 to the Buckeyes (10-1, 7-1). And it could have been more if Davison Igbinosun had kept his hands to himself. (The OSU cornerback drew three pass interference penalties that set up IU touchdowns.)

The Buckeyes weren't perfect. They stalled in the red zone, failed on a fourth-and-1 and still look a little squishy on the offensive line. But they remain better than most, even if they refuse to believe their own headlines.

"I'm never one to be uber-thrilled after a win. That's just not how I'm hardwired," said wide

Tight end Jelani Thurman made his one catch count, hauling in a touchdown in the 38-15 win over upstart Indiana. ADAM CAIRNS/COLUMBUS DISPATCH

receiver Emeka Egbuka, whose seven catches led OSU. "We get in the red zone, fourth-and-1, we have to convert that 10 out of 10 times, no matter who lines up against us."

But especially if the "who" is Michigan. Most of us have witnessed enough OSU-UM games to know that missed scoring opportunities come back to haunt.

"And we can't have a turnover in the red zone, ever," Egbuka added.

"Ever" includes this coming Saturday. Cough up the ball to Michigan near the goal line and it might not matter that the Wolverines are 6-5 after a 50-6 win over Northwestern. The Buckeyes have blown games to worse UM teams. Google it.

Indiana coach has to eat his words

Speaking of, Indiana coach Curt Cignetti, who once said "Google me. I win," is now 0-1 against Ohio State. Google him. He loses, too. (Cignetti also said late last year while addressing an IU basketball crowd that OSU "sucks," but don't destroy him for that bit of brazen bravado. Someone needed to fire up sleepy Hoosiers fans.)

Egbuka did not want to talk about the Michigan "narrative" beyond the obligatory "it's a big game" company line. But safe to say he did not return for a fifth season just to miss out on another chance to collect a gold pants charm.

Ohio State quarterback Will Howard was more primed to discuss the rivalry game, perhaps because he has never played in one. After apologizing for calling "The Team Up North" by its given name, Howard spoke passionately about wanting to beat you-know-who for teammates who have never experienced a win over the maize and blue.

"From the moment I got here, I don't wear blue. And it's beat The Team Up North," said Howard, who made a few poor decisions against the Hoosiers but mostly was on top of his game, completing 22 of 26

passes for 201 yards and two touchdowns with an interception in the red zone.

Is Ohio State good enough to win it all?

I asked Howard and Egbuka if the team that dismantled Indiana is good enough to beat not only Michigan but anyone else.

"I don't want to say yes or no to that, because we're going to need to turn it up," Howard said, adding that "we're picking up momentum at the right time."

Howard then offered a you-ain't-seen-nothing-yet addendum to his comments: "I still don't think you've seen our best."

Maybe not, but this one was OSU's most complete game of the season. Sure, the run game was only so-so as it adjusts to operating behind a repurposed line that is only adequate, but most everything else clicked into place. The defense gave up a combined total of 145 yards on IU's first and last drives, but only six yards in between. Yikes. Defensive coordinator Jim Knowles increasingly is giving his best players freedom to wreak havoc, and the results are impressive. The Buckeyes registered five sacks and limited the nation's second-ranked scoring offense (43.9 points) to 15 points.

Ohio State's offense put up 31 points on the nation's seventh-ranked scoring defense, and for the second straight week OSU took advantage of an opponent's punt team miscue to set up short-field touchdowns.

Then there was Caleb Downs, who returned a punt 79 yards for a touchdown, and barely broke a sweat doing so. Downs made his return, which put OSU ahead 21-7 early in the second half, appear ridiculously effortless.

Buckeyes clicking on offense, defense and special teams

Put the three phases together — offense, defense and special teams — and Ohio State is trending toward

Emeka Egbuka paced Ohio State with seven catches for 80 yards and a touchdown in the win over the previously unbeaten Hoosiers. ADAM CAIRNS/COLUMBUS DISPATCH

making a deep run in the College Football Playoff.

Are the Buckeyes great? No. But they are very good most everywhere, with the exception of the offensive line, which could pose a problem against Michigan.

Howard closed his interview session with this nugget: "When you go into that locker room and look into the eyes of every single guy, you see the edge."

The edge. These Buckeyes have elite skill players, but top-level talent is not enough to win championships, as proved the past three seasons. You also need attitude, or edge. At times, you need to score a touchdown instead of taking a knee. Ohio State has lacked edge in recent years. We're about to find out how much that has changed.

Ryan Day is now 4-6 against top-five teams, but that means nothing if OSU can't close the deal against Michigan. If the Buckeyes play like

they did against Indiana, it should be enough. If they play even a little better than they did against the Hoosiers, it might just end with a national championship.

"We have all the resources to win it all," Egbuka said.

But first they must beat Michigan. Buckle up, Buckeyes fans. The answer to "can they?" comes in less than a week. ■

November 30, 2024 • Columbus, Ohio

'I'M SORRY'

Howard's Interceptions Doom Ohio State in Another Loss to Michigan

By Joey Kaufman

Will Howard was instrumental in leading Ohio State to two top-five wins over Indiana and Penn State earlier in November.

But in the game the Buckeyes needed in order to snap a painful losing streak to their archrival and reach the Big Ten championship game, the veteran quarterback cost them with turnovers.

Howard threw two interceptions Saturday that doomed the Buckeyes in an inexplicable 13-10 loss to unranked Michigan that marked their fourth straight defeat to the Wolverines, their longest losing streak in The Game in more than three decades.

It left him choking up as he stood in front of a room of reporters and TV cameras afterward.

"I'm blessed to have the opportunity to be a Buckeye," Howard said, "and I'm sorry I couldn't get this one done."

Since he transferred to Ohio State from Kansas State for his final season of eligibility, Howard had not been picked off more than once in a game.

Throughout the fall, he had proven himself a savvy decision-maker from the pocket and looked like a clear upgrade over Kyle McCord, who started behind center for the Buckeyes last season before transferring to Syracuse.

Entering the final weekend of the regular season, Howard had the highest completion percentage among qualifying passers in the Football Bowl Subdivision.

But in a sequence that mirrored McCord's start to the rivalry game last November, Howard threw an early pick that set up a touchdown for the Wolverines.

With the Buckeyes facing a third-and-9 from their 4-yard line in the opening minutes of the second quarter, Howard looked to sophomore receiver Carnell Tate running an out route on the short side of the field when cornerback Aamir Hall jumped the route and snagged an interception.

"I've got to keep it outside," Howard said. "I can't make that play."

Hall returned the interception to Ohio State's 2-yard line, allowing Michigan to turn to running back Kalel Mullings on consecutive carries. Mullings' second broke the goal line for a score that put the Wolverines ahead by a score of 7-3. They never trailed again.

Howard would play through pain against the Wolverines. He was sidelined later in the second

Quarterback Will Howard had a tough day against Michigan, completing just 19 of 33 passes for 175 yards, one touchdown and two damaging interceptions. ADAM CAIRNS/COLUMBUS DISPATCH

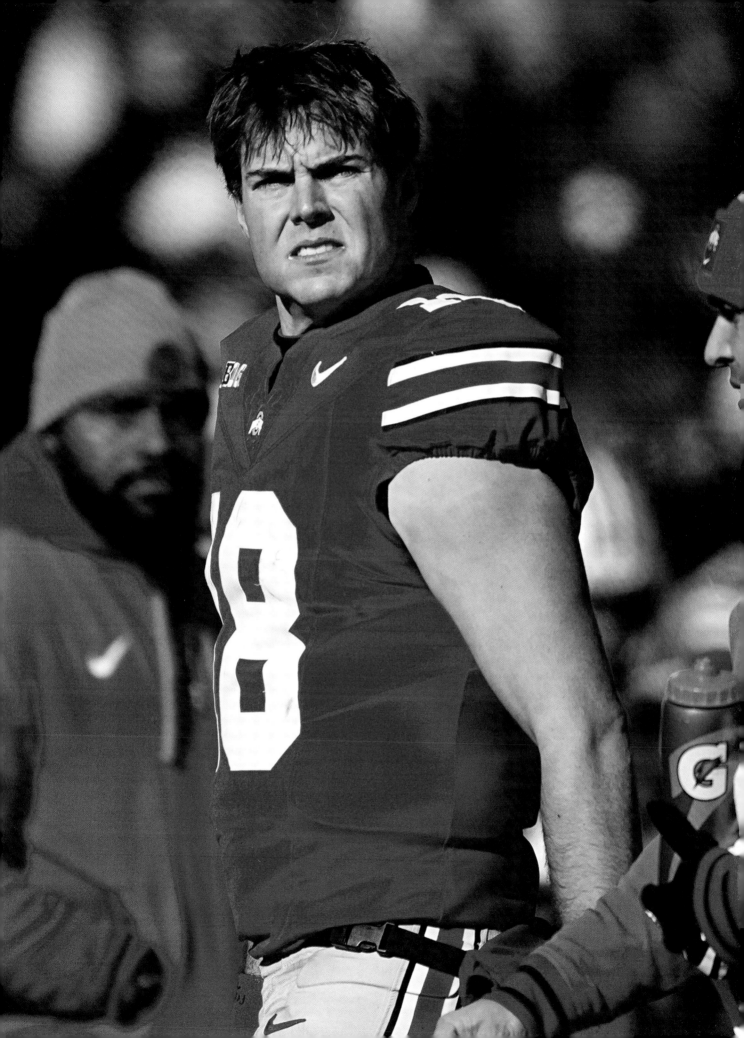

quarter after taking a hard hit while looking to run for a first down.

With Howard within of yard of moving the chains, safety Makari Paige lowered his shoulder and knocked him down at the Wolverines' 33-yard line.

While trainers evaluated him on the sideline, backup Devin Brown replaced him on fourth down and handed the ball off to running back Quinshon Judkins, who ran for 10 yards to continue the drive.

"It was my head," Howard said, "and I was good enough to come back."

Buckeyes coach Ryan Day said that, after Judkins' run, Howard was cleared by the medical staff to return. Howard sat out just the one play.

"I just go based off what our doctors say," Day said. "He came out for a second, and they said he was available and OK to go back into the game. I checked with him. He said he was in good shape."

Howard's next three passes fell incomplete before he led the Buckeyes on a touchdown drive late in the second quarter that would tie the score at 10 apiece, finding freshman receiver Jeremiah Smith in the end zone for a 10-yard touchdown with 30 seconds left until halftime.

Howard, who completed 19 of 33 passes for a season-low 175 yards, threw his second interception late in the third quarter after the Buckeyes had reached Michigan's 16-yard line and faced a third-and-7, killing a potential scoring drive.

With Emeka Egbuka open between two defenders past the first-down marker, Howard attempted to squeeze a pass into his grasp. Only it was snagged by Paige, who trailed Egbuka.

"I was just a little behind on the throw," Howard said.

The turnover kept the Buckeyes from at least attempting a field goal, though points were no guarantee. Kicker Jayden Fielding made a 29-yard field goal to end Ohio State's first possession, then he missed from 34 and 38 yards.

"I know he's trying to make a play on third down in the red zone," Day said, "and probably could've just thrown that away and we had a field-goal opportunity there. There's a fine line of trying to make plays and win the game and also being smart enough to take care of the ball. That's the balance of trying to play quarterback.

"I think we all know that Will gave everything he possibly had today."

While the Buckeyes still figure to be bound for the College Football Playoff after ending the regular season with a 10-2 record, it did little to console Howard, who fell short in his first and only appearance in The Game.

When asked where Ohio State's postseason fate ranked among his thoughts given all that had transpired earlier Saturday, Howard was succinct.

"Very low," he said. ∎

Will Howard can only watch as Michigan celebrates a fourth-down stop late in the game to seal the upset over the Buckeyes. ADAM CAIRNS/COLUMBUS DISPATCH

Latest Loss to Michigan the Most Shocking Yet

By Bill Rabinowitz

Ohio State football fans awoke Sunday and realized it wasn't just a bad dream.

The Buckeyes really had lost to Michigan — again — and this fourth straight loss was by far the most painful. There was no rationalizing this one the way it was possible for the first two when Connor Stalions was stealing OSU's signs. The Buckeyes didn't lose on the road to the eventual national champions as they did last year.

This was a rebuilding Michigan team with a feeble passing game missing its top target, tight end Colston Loveland. Quarterback Davis Warren threw for only 62 yards and was intercepted twice.

Yet somehow the No. 2 Buckeyes (10-2, 7-2) squandered many chances to take control of the game. This 13-10 loss will haunt forever.

Ohio State's seniors returned for a final season largely to get redemption against the Wolverines (7-5, 5-4). Coach Ryan Day badly needed a win to quiet the skeptics. Yes, it's nice to beat Penn State and Indiana, but Michigan is the essential one.

And the Buckeyes blew it. This was a failure in all three phases. Why did Day and offensive coordinator Chip Kelly insist on running the ball into the teeth of Michigan's stout defensive front when that matchup against Ohio State's makeshift offensive line was one of the only that favored the Wolverines?

Ohio State ran 26 times for 77 yards, and that number includes a 17-yarder by Quinshon Judkins.

Quarterback Will Howard threw two awful interceptions, one that set up Michigan's only touchdown and the other in the red zone when the game was tied. Ohio State didn't score in the second half and didn't have a first down for almost the final 21 minutes of the game. How is that possible with the players OSU has?

Ohio State's special teams were a disaster. Jayden Fielding missed field goals of 34 and 38 yards. Either could have been the difference. Michigan counterpart Dominic Zvada made a 54-yarder.

TreVeyon Henderson misplayed the second-half kickoff and recovered at the 6, putting the Buckeyes in a hole from the start. Even Caleb Downs let a punt bounce. It became a 68-yarder that flipped the field.

The defense did its part until the end. On Michigan's final drive, it had Kalel Mullings seemingly hemmed in on a third-and-6 before he broke free for a 27-yard gain. Then Ohio State committed an illegal substitution penalty for having 12 men on the field, which gave Michigan a first down and allowed the Wolverines to bleed the clock before Zvada's chip-shot game-winning field goal. Day attributed the penalty to panic by the Buckeyes.

So where do the Buckeyes go from here? Well, not to Indianapolis. Ohio State's chance for its first Big Ten title since 2020 was gone.

Can Ohio State still make the College Football Playoff? It's not guaranteed

The Buckeyes now must wait a week to learn their College Football Playoff fate. OSU is a virtual lock to be in the 12-team field. It is likely to host a first-round game in three weeks at the Horseshoe, depending on how the conference title games play out. The Buckeyes' unofficial motto this year is "Natty or bust," and that remains attainable.

Ohio State has time to regroup, and that task will be the ultimate test of its coaches and leaders. They must drown out the noise, which will be considerable. The Buckeyes did so two years ago when they played inspired in a heartbreaking 42-41 loss to Georgia in the CFP semifinals.

Day's record is 66-10, but that's of little importance to the Buckeyes fans who find the Michigan losses, especially this one, unforgivable. Day has said repeatedly he knew from the day he took the job that beating Michigan was the top priority.

Athletic director Ross Bjork declines to comment about Ryan Day's future

First-year athletic director Ross Bjork declined to comment when asked about Day's status. As much as a part of the OSU fan base would like Day fired, it's not so simple. Day would be owed a hefty buyout at a time when athletic departments are strapped by the imminent demands of revenue sharing with players.

Also, early signing day is Wednesday. Ohio State has a top-three class, according to 247Sports. A coaching change, or even uncertainty about it, could be devastating.

These days, all college programs are a house of cards to some degree because of the transfer portal. Ohio State benefited this year when Downs and center Seth McLaughlin left Alabama for Columbus following Nick Saban's retirement.

The Buckeyes could face an exodus if Day leaves. Ohio State has five blue-chip quarterbacks on its roster. If he leaves, would any of them stay? Would Downs or star freshman receiver Jeremiah Smith?

Who could be next in line as OSU coach if Day gets fired?

As for possible successors, there is no Urban Meyer on the market like in 2011 after Jim Tressel's firing. Luke Fickell's star has faded after two disappointing

seasons at Wisconsin. Some fans might covet Mike Vrabel, but few NFL coaches want to deal with the college landscape as it is now. There is no obvious heir apparent on the current staff.

The flip side to the Day issue is whether he wants to stay. He said last week that losing to Michigan is the worst thing that's happened to his family. Hopefully, decency will prevail and even those who want Day gone will leave his family alone. But is decency even a thing anymore?

All of this leaves Ohio State in a precarious state. If the Buckeyes can make a long run in the playoff, perhaps the pain and frustration will ease. If not, this becomes a program at a crossroads, which seemed unimaginable before a shocking loss. ■

Flag-Planting Brawl Punctuates Brutal Buckeyes Loss

By Jordan Laird

After Michigan defeated Ohio State for the fourth straight season, a melee broke out on the field that cost the universities $100,000 each and embroiled them in a national debate about sportsmanship.

Here's the play-by-play of what happened.

After the game ended, Buckeyes coach Ryan Day and Wolverines coach Sherrone Moore shook hands at midfield.

The Ohio State players and coaching staff, including Day, gathered in front of the South Stands for the postgame tradition of singing "Carmen Ohio."

While the band still was playing, Wolverines players headed to midfield to celebrate. The players had multiple Michigan flags with them and tried to plant a large flag inside the center of the Block O.

The Wolverines mimed planting their flag in the turf as OSU players approached. Police officers and some others appeared to attempt to hold the players back but were unsuccessful.

A chaotic scuffle involving scores of players ensued. After about 30 seconds, these skirmishes were broken up and the teams milled on the field.

There was about 30 seconds of relative calm, but UM defensive end Derrick Moore still was parading a large flag around the field.

Ohio State defensive end Jack Sawyer grabbed the flag, ripped it off its pole and threw it to the turf as the crowd in the Horseshoe cheered.

This led to more fighting between the teams.

Amid this second wave of fighting, it was later determined that three officers — one from each of the policing agencies on the field — deployed pepper spray on several players from each team. Bodycam footage also revealed that officers used the threat of Tasers, including one deputy who pressed his stun gun into a Michigan player's back.

Officers were present from the Ohio State University Police, University of Michigan Police and Franklin County Sheriff's Office. A U-M officer, according to Dispatch photos and videos, appeared to be the first to use pepper spray. Defensive lineman Kayden McDonald appeared to take the brunt of the spray and was helped off the field by teammates.

Still, it wasn't long before staff for each team and a large number of officers managed to get between the teams. Then the teams headed to their locker rooms.

The whole incident lasted less than four minutes.

But it would dominate the sports world for days.

No arrests were made or citations issued. The next day, the Big Ten fined each team $100,000. OSU police took the lead in investigating who did what and when and why.

As expected, social media blew up over the incident. Day's actions — actually his inaction — became a meme. Fox's cameras showed Day standing far from the skirmishes with an expression variously described as stone-faced or dazed or blank or frozen.

Afterward, Day told the media: "I don't know all the details of it, but I know that these guys are looking to put a flag on our field and our guys weren't going to let that happen. I'll find out exactly what happened. But this is our field. Certainly, we're embarrassed of the fact that we lost the game, but there's some prideful guys in this team that weren't going to just let that happen."

Moore said: "I did see they had the flag and guys were waving it around and their guys charged us. There's emotion on both sides. It can't happen." ∎

Shahid Meighan, Bailey Gallion, Sheridan Hendrix and Tony Garcia contributed.

Ohio State defensive end Jack Sawyer tosses the Michigan flag after it was planted at midfield by victorious Wolverines players in an ugly postgame scene. BARBARA J. PERENIC/COLUMBUS DISPATCH

THE GLORY

E SANFORD TROPHY
OUTSTANDING OFFENSIVE PLAYER

COLLEGE FOOTBALL PLAYOFF FIRST ROUND

NO. 8 SEED OHIO STATE 42, NO. 9 SEED TENNESSEE 17
December 21, 2024 • Columbus, Ohio

SILENCING THE CRITICS

Ryan Day Does About-Face, Opens Up OSU Offense vs. Vols

By Rob Oller

Ryan Day just led the Buckeyes to the most important win of his career. Because it wasn't a loss.

If Ohio State had stumbled hard against Tennessee on Saturday night in the scarlet-and-orange infused Horseshoe — and especially if the loss was like the abomination against Michigan three weeks ago — the torch and pitchfork-carrying crowd among Buckeye Nation would have made a beeline down High Street, turned left down Lane Avenue and, after navigating dejected OSU tailgaters and dodging ebullient Volunteers fans, searched every room of the stadium to find Day and run Ohio State's coach out on a rail.

OSU athletic director Ross Bjork is unlikely to have held the door open for the angry mob and disaffected donors. After the Michigan loss, Bjork gave his 45-year-old coach what sounded like a vote of confidence on steroids.

"He's our coach," Bjork said.

But would Bjork have slammed the door in the mob's face and bolted it shut? Doubtful. After all, "He's our coach" is not time sensitive. One day he is and the next he's not.

It's one thing to support your coach, as Bjork has done. It's quite another to go to the mat for him, because you might get pinned yourself by FOPs (Friends of the Program) in even higher tax brackets.

Ryan Day pulls 180 from Michigan to Tennessee

The good news for Bjork is we'll never know, because Day pulled a 180 against the Vols, opening up the Buckeyes' offense. It was the opposite of how he and play-caller Chip Kelly closed things down in the 13-10 loss to the Wolverines on Nov. 30.

Instead of playing Woody ball by repeatedly running it up the gut, Day switched to "backyard ball," which anyone who has squeezed a Nerf football knows means tossing it here, there and everywhere.

Day did to Tennessee what he should have done to Michigan, by unveiling a game plan that used the pass to set up the run. And by the time the clock struck midnight, his job status no longer felt as if it was on shaky ground.

Let me be clear: I never thought Day would lose his job if he lost to Tennessee, at least not if OSU lost a close one and the Buckeyes looked competent. A blowout loss, however, and all bets were off.

That's why dominating Tennessee 42-17 was so huge for Day, even bigger than it was for the Buckeyes. It not only got him one more game without flaming darts whizzing past his ears, but it showed that when he trusts his instincts and stays aggressive instead of going into a shell, like whatever that was against Michigan, his teams almost always

TreVeyon Henderson had a big game in the win against the Vols with 10 rushes for 80 yards and two touchdowns, as well as four catches for 54 yards. ADAM CAIRNS/COLUMBUS DISPATCH

are in the hunt, if not always victorious. Against Georgia two years ago, and against Clemson in 2020, Day went all-in by letting his offense fly. The Buckeyes clubbed Clemson 49-28 and took eventual national champion Georgia to the final second before losing on a missed field goal.

It's probably true that Michigan is in Day's head, but an easy way to get the Wolverines out of there is to lean into your identity. And OSU's identity since Day took over from Urban Meyer in 2019 is to pair elite wide receivers with above-average quarterbacks and hope the defense is stout enough to spell the difference, which tends to be more often than not, though not often enough to have secured a national title.

Buckeyes best when they play fast and cut loose

When Day cuts it loose, as he did against Tennessee (10-3), the Buckeyes (11-2) are extremely dangerous. Oregon is about to discover as much. The Ducks are next on OSU's agenda with a rematch in the Rose Bowl set for Jan. 1, 2025.

Prediction: No. 8 seed Ohio State, bubbling with confidence after demolishing Rocky Top, will upset No. 1 seed Oregon in Pasadena. It won't be easy, and the outcome won't be determined until after the sun sets on the San Gabriel Mountains early in the fourth quarter, but the 32-31 loss in Eugene on Oct. 12 will be avenged. Book it.

Back to discussing Day's job security. Tennessee was always going to be a program-defining game for the Buckeyes and their coach. But only if they lost. A win simply would mean getting another bite at the apple, and a juicy one at that.

Beat Oregon and the "Is Day right for the job?" debate will die down faster than a political argument at the Christmas dinner table. Not now, family.

But a CFP loss Saturday would have jacked the "Fire Day" speaker knob to 11. And a bad loss would have broken the Internet.

Returning to Bjork's comments three weeks ago,

the AD addressed whether public opinion might sway him to rescind his support of Day.

"Let's go make a run in the playoff," he said. "That's all I'm going to say. Let's go make a run in the playoff. That's what we've got to do."

What defines a run? One win? Two? Winning the natty? Only Bjork knows, but you have to think that the way Day turned things around after Michigan endeared him to his boss and other university/community bigwigs. If nothing else, it showed that Day is teachable.

I asked Day postgame what changed from a coaching perspective from Michigan to Tennessee.

"I think it was a combination of things. I think it's a little bit of everything," he said, explaining that OSU was not at its best even before Michigan. "We really didn't play great on offense in the Indiana game, truth be told. And then we went into the (Michigan) game and there was a lot that played into that, but certainly we called this game more aggressively.

"But also we did some things in this game that maximized what we have in terms of our strengths and minimized our deficiencies."

Day praised quarterback Will Howard, who after playing his worst game of the season against Michigan bounced back with one of his best performances, completing 24 of 29 passes for 311 yards, two touchdowns and an interception. It helped immensely that the Buckeyes' offensive line protected him by not allowing a sack.

Mostly, though, the difference this night was Day.

"We had balance in this game," he said, never wanting to be thought of only as a pass-happy coach, a label he has fought for a few years. "It's not like we were just throwing it all over the place. We did get some runs that hit for us, and that makes a big difference when you have that run-pass balance."

No, no, no, coach. Get it right. It's *pass*-run balance. The pass comes first. Remember that. Otherwise, your critics will run, run, run you out of town. ∎

Jeremiah Smith kept up his outstanding play on the big stage with six catches for 103 yards and two touchdowns in the dominant win. SAMANTHA MADAR/COLUMBUS DISPATCH

Inspired by Game Plan, Howard Nearly Flawless in CFP Rout

By Bill Rabinowitz

Will Howard would never be one to say he had qualms about a game plan.

But the Ohio State quarterback had a particularly good feeling before Saturday night's first-round College Football Playoff game against Tennessee.

The Buckeyes had three weeks off since their loss to Michigan, ample time to dissect the Volunteers.

"Having the two or three weeks that we had to get ready for these guys gave us a little bit of an edge," Howard said. "We were able to really break them down and figure out what we liked, what we didn't like, and figure out what we were doing well. Coming into this game, I was really fired up about the game plan more than usual."

Howard and his teammates executed the plan to perfection in the first quarter and then applied the hammer in the second half in the Buckeyes' 42-17 thrashing of the Volunteers at Ohio Stadium.

Howard was 24 of 29 for 311 yards and two touchdowns, both to Jeremiah Smith on deep fade passes in the end zone. Howard completed passes to eight receivers, including himself on a batted ball.

"I thought Will was excellent in this game," Ohio State coach Ryan Day said. "He played really well. He did a really good job of placing the ball on some big-time throws. When he needed to, he made plays with his legs."

Howard ran five times for 37 yards.

It was a nice rebound after the Kansas State transfer threw two costly interceptions in Ohio State's 13-10 loss to Michigan. Tennessee intercepted Howard once, which came on a deflected pass to Smith in the end zone with Ohio State leading 21-0 and trying to land a knockout blow.

Day had no issue with Howard's throw.

"When you're going to call the game aggressively and something like this happens," Day said, "you have to be willing to live with it."

After that interception, Howard completed his next 10 passes. With his 83% completion percentage, Saturday marked the seventh time this season he'd completed 80% or more of his passes.

"He was accurate today," Day said. "A big thing for Will is his footwork. When his footwork's on point and when he's seeing things well, he's as good as anybody in the country."

With the playmakers Ohio State has at receiver in Smith, Emeka Egbuka and Carnell Tate, as well as TreVeyon Henderson and Quinshon Judkins out of the backfield, Howard's job can look easy. It certainly did against Tennessee.

"As a quarterback, you get into a rhythm and get into a flow state," Howard said. "I felt like tonight we were able to get into that." ■

The Buckeyes and Will Howard bounced back after the tough Michigan loss and booked a trip to the Rose Bowl in the process. SAMANTHA MADAR/COLUMBUS DISPATCH

COLLEGE FOOTBALL PLAYOFF ROSE BOWL

NO. 8 SEED OHIO STATE 41, NO. 1 SEED OREGON 21

January 1, 2025 • Pasadena, California

ATTITUDE ADJUSTMENT

OSU's Defense Gets Redemption After Struggles in October's Loss

By Bill Rabinowitz

His fiancée at his side, defensive coordinator Jim Knowles beamed as he walked to the Ohio State bus.

Cornerback Denzel Burke, who had a nightmarish game against Oregon in October, held a rose in his hand and wore a smile as big as Knowles'.

Ohio State's 41-21 College Football Playoff quarterfinal victory at the Rose Bowl over the top-seeded Ducks was special for all the Buckeyes, but maybe meant the most to these two. Ohio State's defense is the top-ranked one in the country, but that 32-31 loss at Autzen Stadium cut deep.

"It bothered me for the players," Knowles said. "They've been really good all year, (actually) great. They had one game where they had some bad plays. It was tough on me. You feel like a parent who sees people get down on them.

"I'm just so happy for them that they were able to come back and have a dominating effort."

Oregon has the two highest-scoring outings against Ohio State this season, but its 21 points New Year's Day came after Ohio State had built a 34-0 lead. At that point, the Buckeyes had allowed only 64 yards on six Oregon possessions.

Eighth-seeded Ohio State (12-2) swarmed Oregon's running game. The Ducks averaged 1.7 yards on their 20 carries. Jordan James, who gained 115 yards in the first meeting, was knocked out of the game after managing only 14 yards on seven carries. Quarterback Dillon Gabriel, who finished third in the Heisman Trophy voting and had torched the Buckeyes in the game at Autzen Stadium, was sacked eight times. Several of the 5-foot-11 quarterback's passes were batted down.

"We presented different looks," Knowles said, "and that's what made the quarterback hold the ball. And we shut down the run early, and that (made them one-dimensional), and that helped us."

An explosive offense all season, Oregon (13-1) didn't have a play longer than 12 yards until connecting on a 44-yarder to set up its first touchdown at the end of the first half.

When the Ducks opened the third quarter with another touchdown drive, it looked like the second half might not be a formality, after all.

But the Buckeyes would have none of it. Defensive end Jack Sawyer and linebacker Cody Simon had sacks to force a three-and-out on Oregon's next possession. When the offense scored, the game was essentially over.

Sawyer, fellow defensive end J.T. Tuimoloau and Simon each had two sacks. Simon had 11 tackles and was selected the game's outstanding defensive player.

"One of the biggest things we changed was our attitude and mentality," Simon said. "There were plays in the game when we weren't aligned or ready

Emeka Egbuka celebrates his 42-yard touchdown catch with quarterback Will Howard in the first half of the Rose Bowl against unbeaten and top-seeded Oregon. ADAM CAIRNS/COLUMBUS DISPATCH

to go. With an offense like that for Oregon, they thrive on that stuff.

"For us, it was just that mentality we had to change. We went through a lot of tough conversations after that game and a lot of changes we had to make, but I think we're better for it now."

The pressure on Gabriel was so constant that he didn't have much chance to throw it downfield. Burke was targeted only once, and he had that deep ball well defended. If it hadn't been overthrown for an incompletion, he said he would have intercepted it.

Burke said during the week that it took him a while to get over that October game. He and his teammates got their redemption in a game that mattered more.

"It's a blessing, a blessing in disguise," he said. "Everything happened how it's supposed to happen." ∎

Above: Linebacker Cody Simon (0) celebrates one of his two sacks with teammate Ty Hamilton (58). ADAM CAIRNS/COLUMBUS DISPATCH

Opposite: TreVeyon Henderson streaks for one of his two touchdowns as Ohio State avenged its early season Big Ten loss to Oregon. ADAM CAIRNS/ COLUMBUS DISPATCH

Down go the Ducks! Five Truths We Learned from the Rose Bowl

By Joey Kaufman

ere are five things we learned from No. 8 Ohio State's 41-21 win over No. 1 Oregon in their College Football Playoff quarterfinal.

For Ohio State, momentum is real

Two days before the Rose Bowl, it was Buckeyes coach Ryan Day who acknowledged momentum as a potential factor.

He pointed to wild-card playoff teams in the NFL who got hot after prevailing in the opening round, kick-starting a postseason run.

Day turned out prophetic.

As the Buckeyes opened with an onslaught, finishing with points on six of their first seven drives, the barrage in the first half seemed to be a carryover from their rout of Tennessee less than two weeks ago.

Ohio State was off for only 10 days between games, while Oregon experienced a layoff twice as long. The Ducks had been off for 24 days following the Big Ten championship game on Dec. 7.

It's clear the Buckeyes are peaking at the right time, emerging as the juggernaut they were forecast to be during the offseason. In two playoff games, they have outscored opponents 83-38.

As they move on to the semifinals, they look like the hottest team in the field.

Jeremiah Smith is driving the bus

If Smith ever hit a freshman wall this season, he smashed through it.

Smith was again the focal point of Ohio State's scoring surge, catching two touchdown passes in his second straight playoff game.

Quarterback Will Howard targeted Smith 10 times. He caught seven passes for 187 yards and two scores.

Smith stressed the Ducks in a variety of ways. His touchdown on the opening series came when he got the ball while running a crossing route behind the line of scrimmage and took off for a 45-yard touchdown, showing a burst of speed after the catch.

He later used his size to leap over two defenders for a 29-yard catch on their next possession.

"He's special," offensive coordinator Chip Kelly said. "I've said it from the beginning, I've not seen anybody like him. That combination of size and speed, the ability to track the football, the ability to go up and get the football, he's maybe a once-in-a-lifetime guy."

He could carry the Buckeyes to a title if he continues this stretch of dominance.

Improved defense not an illusion

When the Buckeyes lost at Oregon on Oct. 12, it was a low point for a defense that allowed a season-high 32 points.

Quarterback Dillon Gabriel torched OSU, navigating the pocket with ease and throwing deep bombs to Tez Johnson and Even Stewart.

The setback prompted the Buckeyes to make adjustments on defense to improve the pass rush and limit big plays.

Coach Ryan Day and the Buckeyes were all smiles, and showered by confetti, after winning the Rose Bowl with a dominant performance. ADAM CAIRNS/COLUMBUS DISPATCH

During the second half of the season, their defensive starters had not allowed more than a touchdown.

The rematch with the Ducks revealed the changes had fixed their issues.

Ohio State swarmed Gabriel, sacking him eight times and allowing him to connect on only two passes longer than 25 yards. Gabriel had completed six passes of at least 25 yards, including touchdowns of 48 and 69 yards to Johnson and Stewart, in their first meeting.

Jordan James, who ran for 115 yards and a touchdown previously against the Buckeyes, had only 14 rushing yards on seven carries before he left with an injury in the second quarter.

The Ducks were held to minus-23 rushing yards on 28 carries.

"It's always a test," defensive coordinator Jim Knowles, "and to go against somebody you didn't play well, it's a good feeling."

Fielding snaps slump at right time

There are limitations with Jayden Fielding, who has handled the kicking for the Buckeyes for the past two seasons.

Having never made a 50-yard field goal, he has not been known for his leg.

But he has been accurate and made 25 of his first 30 attempts with the Buckeyes until the loss to Michigan in November that saw him miss two within 40 yards.

That made his two successful tries from 46 and 36 yards against the Ducks valuable, providing some confidence as the Buckeyes move deeper into the postseason.

It stands to reason that a semifinal against Texas on Jan. 10 or a potential final against Notre Dame or Penn State could be tight.

A semifinal loss to the Bulldogs two seasons ago came down to a 50-yard field goal attempt by Noah Ruggles.

Ohio State might need to rely on Fielding. It couldn't afford for him to go into the tank.

Pasadena still friendly turf for OSU

During a stretch in the 1970s, the Buckeyes saw four potential national championship-winning seasons collapse in the Rose Bowl.

They were in position to win it all during the 1970, 1974, 1975 and 1979 seasons until losses on New Year's Day cost them.

Before a win over Arizona State in the 1997 Rose Bowl, they had dropped four in a row and six of seven in the Granddaddy of Them All.

The San Gabriel Mountains did not always look so picturesque to those visiting from Ohio.

But the triumph over Arizona State from 28 years ago remains a turning point. The Buckeyes have won five consecutive games in Pasadena, their longest streak in the history of the historic bowl.

Two of those five wins have come in Day's tenure, including a thriller over Utah three years ago. ∎

Jeremiah Smith was selected the Rose Bowl's offensive MVP, just the latest accolade in his memorable freshman campaign. ADAM CAIRNS/COLUMBUS DISPATCH

COLLEGE FOOTBALL PLAYOFF COTTON BOWL

NO. 8 SEED OHIO STATE 28, NO. 5 SEED TEXAS 14
January 10, 2025 • Arlington, Texas

'THEY AIN'T SCORED YET'

Defense Dunks Texas on Memorable Goal-Line Stand Topped by Sawyer TD

By Rob Oller

Jim Knowles was on the phone right before one of the most game-changing plays in Ohio State history hammered itself into Buckeyes lore.

And the OSU defensive coordinator didn't like what he was hearing.

Texas had quickly moved into striking distance, first-and-goal from the Ohio State 1-yard line with 3:56 left in Friday's Cotton Bowl, and someone on OSU's staff — Knowles did not divulge the coach's identity — *assumed* the Longhorns would score to tie things at 21-all.

But Knowles, as stubborn and feisty as the Philadelphia neighborhood he grew up in, disagreed that a Texas touchdown was a foregone conclusion.

"Here's what goes through my head," Knowles said of the seemingly dire situation he was witnessing from the press box coaching booth. "Somebody said on the (sideline) phone, 'Boy, they scored fast there.' And I said, 'They ain't scored yet.'"

They ain't scored yet.

Damn right.

And they didn't. Game. Set. March to Atlanta.

Decades from now, Ohio State fans will rightfully remember Jack Sawyer's 83-yard rumble with the fumble and the way the Buckeyes' senior defensive end huffed and puffed 83 long yards through the heart of the Lone Star State with 2:24

remaining after orchestrating a scoop-and score off a strip-sack of Texas quarterback Quinn Ewers, sealing a 28-14 win. It was a beefy defensive player's version of Zeke Elliott's 85-yard run through the heart of the South in the 2015 Sugar Bowl. Except it took about 10 seconds longer. Maybe 12.

"He was running in slow motion, for sure," OSU freshman wide receiver Jeremiah Smith said, laughing.

If you didn't jump from your seat when Sawyer first hit his former OSU roommate from behind — the two lived together before Ewers transferred to Texas after his freshman season — and then took off for the opposite goal line, you may want to see a doctor. Better yet, an undertaker, because you're already dead. The TD run-turned-walk was as magical a moment as anything seen during the three-different-centuries history of Ohio State football.

But it wasn't the only huge defensive play.

Those who bleed scarlet and gray may forever recall what came two plays before Sawyer's clinching touchdown, which iced the Buckeyes' trip to Atlanta's Mercedes-Benz Stadium for the Jan. 20 national championship game against Notre Dame.

Though not as famous as Sawyer's TD, which linebacker Sonny Styles called "the craziest play

Defensive end Jack Sawyer (33), flanked by safety Sonny Styles (6), rumbles to the end zone after forcing and recovering a fumble on a crucial fourth-quarter fourth down. ADAM CAIRNS/COLUMBUS DISPATCH

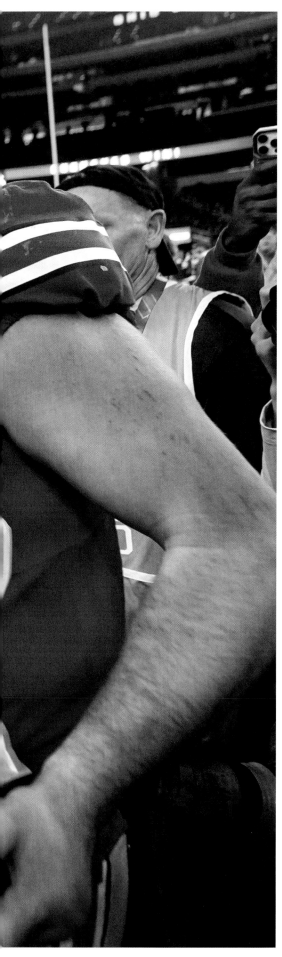

I've ever been a part of in my life," what happened on second-and-goal from the 1 was nearly as vital. OSU safeties Caleb Downs and Lathan Ransom jarred Texas tailback Quintrevion Wisner for a seven-yard loss on a toss sweep that turned a supposedly gimme TD into a slippery downhill 4-footer on third down. It was an odd play call by Longhorns coach Steve Sarkisian, but not so odd that Knowles and the defense managed to sniff it out before the ball was snapped.

"We knew it was coming," defensive end J.T. Tuimoloau said of Texas' toss sweep that backfired. "We had watched film."

Downs echoed his teammate's comment, explaining that he had a feeling Texas would run a sweep, based on "film preparation and feeling the play and the moment. Knowing what they like to do in those moments and believing what we see and pulling our trigger."

Ohio State coach Ryan Day said Knowles went to a "bear" front defense on the play, clogging the interior gaps and forcing the Longhorns to attempt to run wide.

"They tried to stretch the field and it didn't work out for them," defensive tackle Ty Hamilton said.

Sawyer's touchdown and the tackle for loss will take up residence in fans' memories for a long time. What won't be remembered as easily, except by the Buckeyes and their coaches, is what happened on first down from the 1, when Tuimoloau, playing on a sprained ankle, stuffed running back Jerrick Gibson for no gain; and on third down, when Sawyer pressured Ewers' into an incompletion that set up the fourth-down heroics.

But Buckeye Nation should cherish the totality of the four-play goal-line stand, because of what has come before: pain, suffering and here-we-go-again anguish.

Jack Sawyer (33) and Will Howard (18) had a lot of hardware to hold following the Cotton Bowl win over Texas. ADAM CAIRNS/COLUMBUS DISPATCH

For those long enough in the tooth to remember when Ohio Stadium was actually a horseshoe in design and not just name, the story of Ohio State football is one of incredible individual players, yes, but also of "the ones that got away" — the national titles that were lost in large part because the Buckeyes could not get the one essential defensive stop late in the game that would have secured historic hardware.

Brace yourselves, people, this is going to hurt. But the wincing is what makes the Cotton Bowl win all the more enjoyable.

We could go way, way back, but let's start with this: Ohio State failed to corral USC tailback Charles White late in the 1980 Rose Bowl. Get a stop and the Buckeyes win the natty. Instead, White, running primarily behind Anthony Munoz, shredded OSU in the last two minutes in a crushing 17-16 defeat.

There is more in the cobweb closet of Ohio State's Woody-Earle-and-Coop era history, but let's jump way ahead to the 2019 Fiesta Bowl, when Clemson quarterback Trevor Lawrence took the Tigers down the field late in the game for a go-ahead touchdown. Follow that with the 2022 Peach Bowl loss to Georgia, when Ohio State's defense folded down the stretch. Toss in a handful of losses to Michigan since the 1990s and what you come up with are villainous defensive lapses that probably cost the Buckeyes multiple national championships.

Certainly, there are exceptions. Ohio State's defense closed out the 2002 national championship season by stopping Miami (Florida) in the second overtime of the Fiesta Bowl (Aside: the most spectacular defensive play in OSU history was made in that game by an offensive player, when tailback Maurice Clarett stripped the ball from Miami safety Sean Taylor). And those familiar with the name

Cornerback Jordan Hancock takes out Texas running back Quintrevion Wisner, one of Hancock's six tackles in the win. ADAM CAIRNS/COLUMBUS DISPATCH

Griffin may recollect that it was Archie's brother, Ray, who helped save the day with a fourth-quarter interception against the Wolverines in 1975.

But bottom line, the Buckeyes' defense has struggled to make big plays in the biggest games, which is why what happened against Texas was a pinch-me moment to be celebrated on High Street and for thousands of miles beyond.

Ohio State defensive line coach Larry Johnson, who prefers not to reveal his age or birth date — 72 is a pretty safe bet — did willingly reveal his inner child as Sawyer dashed 83 yards down the OSU sideline.

"I started running, clapping, jumping," he said.

The release of emotion was a long time coming. Johnson's reputation as a top defensive line coach is well documented, and he has developed such players as the Bosa brothers, Chase Young, Sam Hubbard and now Sawyer and Tuimoloau into becoming pass rushing royalty. But there also has been an ache for the defense as a whole, a strong desire for the group to come up big, not short, with the game on the line. And get credited for it.

"I thought when it was third down and we got a stop after we got the tackle for loss, and then one more play and all of a sudden there it is," Johnson said.

It. That may be the best word to describe the goal-line stand. Just call it ... it.

"One of our biggest mottos is 'Give us an inch and we'll defend it,'" Styles said.

They did. And it was something to see. ∎

Quarterback Will Howard completed 24 of 33 passes for 289 yards, a touchdown and an interception in the 28-14 win over the Longhorns.
ADAM CAIRNS/COLUMBUS DISPATCH

Inside Sawyer's Play That Put Buckeyes on the Brink of Title

By Joey Kaufman

As Jack Sawyer surged late last season, defensive coordinator Jim Knowles gave him a nickname. Knowles began calling him Mr. November.

"Now we have to add January," Knowles cracked.

In a 28-14 win over Texas that pushed Ohio State into the College Football Playoff final, it was the senior defensive end who stepped up in the clutch.

With the Longhorns facing a fourth-and-goal with 2:29 left, needing only a touchdown to tie the score, Sawyer shot out of his stance along the edge of the line of scrimmage and dipped underneath right tackle Cameron Williams.

As Sawyer burst into the backfield, quarterback Quinn Ewers sought to drift away from the rush before he was smothered.

Sawyer raised his arms while Ewers began attempting a pass, extending enough to knock the ball loose.

"Once he came clear, you can see him change speed to a burst to go for the sack fumble," Ohio State defensive line coach Larry Johnson said. "That's what you do."

The fumble bounced off the AT&T Stadium turf, falling into the grasp of Sawyer at Ohio State's 17-yard line. He never broke stride.

"That's the man above," Johnson said.

As Sawyer secured the ball, he took off, heading 83 yards into the end zone. With a block from linebacker Sonny Styles, boxing out running back Quintrevion Wisner down the sideline, he wasn't caught by any Longhorns.

"I hit about the 30," Sawyer said, "and I looked back, 'I'm like, I hope I get some blockers. I'm running out of steam here.' They were running with me side by side. That speaks volume to who this team is. We always have each other's back."

The touchdown sealed the Buckeyes' semifinal win, a sequence as consequential as any on Friday night.

"It changed the course of the game," Johnson said. "He made the touchdown. It was over."

The fumble return, the longest in the history of the playoff, inspired euphoria among the Buckeyes. As the final seconds wound down, coach Ryan Day leapt into Sawyer's arms in an embrace.

Safety Caleb Downs put a "SportsCenter top-10 chain" around Sawyer's neck during an interview with ESPN.

"That play is iconic," Downs said.

Six weeks earlier, Sawyer had forced another turnover that promised to go down in history, picking off Michigan quarterback Davis Warren at the goal line of the fourth quarter of The Game.

But the Buckeyes could not break the tie, and the Wolverines' next drive saw them kick a game-winning field. As they were ultimately upset, the interception became an afterthought.

Few will forget his scoop-and-score.

"You dream about those plays," linebacker Cody Simon said, "and he made it."

As the Buckeyes continue their postseason run, moving to the precipice of their first national championship in a decade, Sawyer has been one of the most important pieces leading their push.

Over their three playoff wins, he has been

With Texas on the verge of tying the game late in the fourth quarter, Jack Sawyer took things into his own hands by knocking the ball loose from quarterback Quinn Ewers and taking it to the house to all but seal the game for the Buckeyes. ADAM CAIRNS/COLUMBUS DISPATCH

dominant at the line of scrimmage, combining for 4½ sacks and seven pass breakups. Along with his strip-sack against Texas, he often pressured Ewers, getting the better of Williams, the Longhorns' right tackle who returned from a knee injury.

"This is somebody who grew up in Columbus, who has always wanted to be a Buckeye, who has always waited for a moment like this," Day said.

Sawyer was eager enough to end up at Ohio State that he committed to the Buckeyes as a sophomore at Pickerington North High School.

Now he has helped them reached the biggest stage.

"We're going to compete for a national championship," Sawyer said, "which is something I've always dreamed of bringing back to Columbus since I was a little kid, throwing the football in the backyard with my dad with an Ohio State jersey on. I'm just really looking forward to that, and I was fortunate enough to make a big-time play like a lot of guys did." ■

Plagued by Penalties All Game, OSU Clicked for 88-Yard TD Drive

By Bill Rabinowitz

For the Ohio State offense, the moment of truth on a frustrating night came early in the fourth quarter of the Buckeyes' 28-14 College Football Playoff semifinal victory over Texas.

The Longhorns had tied the game at 14. They have one of the top defenses in the country. But Ohio State penalties were mostly responsible for the offense's struggles.

The Buckeyes had an impressive touchdown drive on their first possession and scored on a 75-yard screen to TreVeyon Henderson in the final seconds of the second quarter for a 14-7 halftime lead.

But Henderson had drawn an unsportsmanlike conduct penalty earlier, and holding calls all but killed two subsequent possessions. Guard Austin Siereveld was flagged for a late hit to stall another drive late in the third quarter.

The field had shifted in the Longhorns' favor. The Buckeyes started their next possession at their 12.

But just when things looked bleak, Ohio State responded with a 13-play, 88-yard touchdown drive to take the lead for good.

Carnell Tate had an 18-yard catch on third-and-8, but an even bigger play came on fourth-and-2 from the Texas 34.

Quarterback Will Howard ran for 18 yards and would have scored if he hadn't tripped over his own feet.

"That fourth down was huge," Howard said. "They came out and gave us a good look for the play. The O-line blocked it up well."

As for the stumble, Howard joked, "I fell on purpose. I was trying to keep a couple of seconds on the clock."

The Buckeyes scored four plays later on Quinshon Judkins' 1-yard run for his second touchdown of the game for a 21-14 lead.

"We needed that," Howard said. "We'd been beating ourselves all day with penalties and getting behind the sticks. That was a statement drive. The O-line did a heck of a job on that drive."

That proved to be the decisive score. Later, OSU defensive end Jack Sawyer scored on an 83-yard strip-sack.

It was a game in which little went according to plan on offense. Star freshman wide receiver Jeremiah Smith was a nonfactor because Texas devised a scheme to prevent him from doing what he did in the CFP routs of Tennessee and Oregon. It didn't help that Smith landed hard on his back on his only catch, an early 3-yarder.

Howard was sacked (twice) for the first time in five games.

Even the Henderson touchdown on the screen pass happened almost by accident. Ohio State coach Ryan Day said it had become a joke among the players that the Buckeyes practice screen plays but seldom run them.

When they took over at their 25 with 29 seconds left, Day said coaches debated what to call.

"What do you want to run?" Day said of that conversation. "You want to run the ball? You want to take a knee? I said, 'No, just run the screen.' Sure enough, it went the whole distance."

Henderson caught the ball, followed several blockers and used his speed to break free for a touchdown.

"I don't think anyone thought that was going to go for 75 yards," Day said.

That gave Ohio State a huge momentum boost heading into the second half. But the Buckeyes couldn't sustain it, doing little in the third quarter.

Then came the 88-yard drive that saved their season. ■

While TreVeyon Henderson had a modest day on the ground with just six carries for 42 yards, he made a huge impact through the air with this 75-yard touchdown catch in the second quarter. KYLE ROBERTSON/COLUMBUS DISPATCH

COLLEGE FOOTBALL PLAYOFF NATIONAL CHAMPIONSHIP

NO. 8 SEED OHIO STATE 34, NO. 7 SEED NOTRE DAME 23
January 20, 2025 • Atlanta, Georgia

NO DOUBT ABOUT IT!

Buckeyes Take Big Early Lead and Shut the Door Late on Fighting Irish to Capture First 12-Team College Football Playoff Crown

By Joey Kaufman and Bill Rabinowitz

All season, "Leave no doubt" had been Ohio State's rallying cry. The Buckeyes didn't want to leave their fate to one play or official's call.

Well, the Buckeyes left a little bit of doubt in the College Football Playoff championship game. But for the first time in a decade, the Buckeyes are the kings of college football after holding on to beat Notre Dame 34-23 in front of 77,660 at Mercedes-Benz Stadium in Atlanta.

The Buckeyes led 31-7 before Notre Dame scored two touchdowns and added a pair of two-point conversions to make it a one-possession game with 4:15 left.

But on third-and-11 with 2:45 left, Will Howard connected with Jeremiah Smith for a 57-yard completion to the Fighting Irish 9.

The Irish vowed before the game to stick with their man-to-man coverage. It cost them when it mattered most when Smith got behind Christian Gray. With 26 seconds left, Jayden Fielding clinched the championship with a 33-yard field goal.

Howard completed his first 13 passes and ran for several clutch first downs to earn offensive player of the game honors. He finished 17 of 21 for 231 yards and two touchdowns.

Quinshon Judkins ran for two touchdowns and caught another.

After Notre Dame's opening touchdown drive, the Buckeyes' top-ranked defense allowed 11 yards in the Irish's next four possessions as Ohio State built its 24-point lead. Linebacker Cody Simon, with eight tackles, was the defensive player of the game

Ohio State earned the title

The Buckeyes (14-2) navigated an unprecedented stretch to win the school's seventh national championship.

It took four playoff victories to lift the trophy, including toppling three of the selection committee's five highest-ranked teams.

Their résumé was not spotless. The Buckeyes lost twice during the regular season, including an ugly loss to archrival Michigan. Other champions have run the table during unbeaten seasons, including two this decade.

But no team ever has faced a more difficult path to the top of the sport. When the four-team playoff or Bowl Championship Series crowned champions over the past quarter-century, the formats required contenders to win only one or two postseason games.

Defensive end JT Tuimoloau made his presence felt in the championship game with five tackles, including a sack and two tackles for loss. ADAM CAIRNS/COLUMBUS DISPATCH

The debut of a 12-team structure added two games more for Ohio State, which needed to manage the wear and tear of a longer season and have the resolve to move through each round.

"Our team has come together so well over the last month and a half," coach Ryan Day said.

All four of the Buckeyes' victories during the playoff run were by double digits. They outscored their opponents 145-75. They trailed for only six minutes.

The Buckeyes were battled-tested and spanning the regular season they beat six of the top eight teams. They are the most deserving champion in the sport's history.

Day finally got over the hump

Day can lay claim to being one of the best coaches in the country.

Not only does his .875 winning percentage remain the highest in the Football Bowl Subdivision, but he also has hardware to take home.

With Kirby Smart of Georgia and Dabo Swinney of Clemson, he is one of three active coaches to win a national championship and the first to guide a team through the expanded playoff format.

Since inheriting the program from Urban Meyer six years ago, Day has faced skepticism over his ability to win a title. Up until this season, he had won only one playoff game. Most of his success was confined to the regular season. A stable tenure lacked a landmark accomplishment.

But this run brings a reputation makeover, allowing Day to move into an exclusive coaching club.

It also puts him in secure historical company. He is Ohio State's fifth championship-winning coach and well positioned to become the first since Woody Hayes to win multiple titles.

Quinshon Judkins was dominant against Notre Dame with 11 carries for 100 yards and two touchdowns, as well as two catches for 21 yards and another touchdown. ADAM CAIRNS/COLUMBUS DISPATCH

OSU held the edge at quarterback

Ohio State and Notre Dame were in the market for a transfer quarterback last offseason. But the Irish were on an earlier timeline and moved to land Riley Leonard from Duke, picking him over Will Howard, who was leaving Kansas State for his final year of eligibility.

The decision resulted in Howard remaining available when the Buckeyes mined the portal, allowing them to bring him in to replace Kyle McCord, who transferred to Syracuse.

Howard's strength as a passer was evident against the Irish (14-2), setting a championship game record with his 13 consecutive completions. Had safety Xavier Watts not broken up a pass to running back TreVeyon Henderson late in the second quarter, he would have been perfect in the first half.

Howard's passing, distributing to a talented cast of playmakers, mattered more than Leonard's running that became less effective following the Irish's first drive.

The middle eight edge flipped

Notre Dame had thrived during the middle eight, which consisted of the last four minutes of the second quarter and first four minutes of the third. The Irish outscored Penn State 10-0 during this stretch in the semifinals, setting the stage for a comeback. Among the 134 teams in the Football Bowl Subdivision, the Irish had the widest scoring margin during the middle eight, as noted by the Wall Street Journal.

But it was the Buckeyes who had the advantage in the championship game, outscoring the Irish 14-0 during the stretch, adding to a 14-7 lead that became nearly insurmountable.

Day and offensive coordinator Chip Kelly were aware of the Irish's knack for winning the middle eight. They controlled the tempo on a touchdown drive late in the second quarter, reaching the end zone with only 27 seconds left. That effectively allowed them to steal a possession as they had deferred to the second half and used the opening series to again march down the field, Judkins' 70-yard run setting up another touchdown.

UM no longer defines a season

The stakes of the rivalry with Michigan largely had been all or nothing for more than a century.

A loss to the Wolverines in late November was bound to keep the Buckeyes from winning a national championship. Especially in the poll era, they needed to prevail in The Game to finish atop the Big Ten standings and have a shot at being voted No. 1 by the sportswriters or coaches.

But the expansion of the playoff has changed the tenor of the rivalry.

A setback will cost the Buckeyes bragging rights, as it did this season when they were upset as three-touchdown favorites. But it will not always be a fatal blow.

As long as 12 teams qualify the playoff, Ohio State will be able to withstand losses during the regular season, even ones at the hands of its bitter rival.

For the first time, the Buckeyes have won the national title in a season in which they did not defeat Michigan. ∎

Jeremiah Smith (4) continued his unforgettable and record-setting freshman season with five catches for 88 yards and a touchdown in the win. ADAM CAIRNS/COLUMBUS DISPATCH

OSU Fever Runs High in Bitter Cold as Students Break into Stadium

By Cole Behrens

The bitter cold temperatures in central Ohio didn't keep Ohio State students inside after the Buckeyes secured the national championship.

Within minutes of the clock ticking down on the Buckeyes' 34-23 victory over Notre Dame, students were flooding out across the Columbus campus, quickly making their way to the gates of Ohio Stadium. Temperatures hovered only a few degrees above zero.

Chants of "O-H," "I-O!" rang out as the crowd converged on a shuttered Ohio Stadium. By midnight, students had successfully forced their way into the stadium.

Thomas Schmnasky, a freshman, said he didn't expect to end up on the field at the Horseshoe after the game.

"It's really kind of surreal," he said.

Natalie Freihammer, a senior, said the national championship victory was especially exciting for students who hadn't seen a victory over Michigan. Still, she was amazed how far the celebration went.

"It's crazy," she said. "I was surprised that the cops are so supportive."

Police officers in the stadium also appeared to be enjoying the atmosphere after fans made it inside. Some took videos and photos of fans who asked them to.

By about 12:20 a.m., most students had started filing out. ∎

Opposite: Wide receivers Jeremiah Smith (4) and Carnell Tate (17) celebrate Smith's touchdown to get the Buckeyes on the board early in the second quarter. ADAM CAIRNS/COLUMBUS DISPATCH

Above: Ohio State students stormed Ohio Stadium after the Buckeyes won the national title. COLE BEHRENS/COLUMBUS DISPATCH

'It's an Even Better Story': Day Savors Finally Winning It All

By Bill Rabinowitz

Ryan Day entered the College Football Playoff title game with the highest winning percentage among active coaches.

But it was the 10 losses in those six seasons that largely defined him and haunted him.

The CFP semifinal losses to Clemson in 2019 and Georgia in 2022. Of course, the four straight losses to Michigan.

Woody Hayes won a title in his fourth season at Ohio State, Jim Tressel in his second, Urban Meyer in his third. Day, 45, wondered whether his time would come.

It did with Ohio State's 34-21 victory over Notre Dame at Mercedes-Benz Stadium in Atlanta. Day became a national championship coach.

"This game can give you the highest of highs and the lowest of lows," Day said afterward. "It can take you to your knees some days as a player and as a coach. I've been there before.

"You think back when we were in the stadium last time. I couldn't quite come to grips for a while with why we just didn't quite finish that game against Georgia. But I understand now. It all makes sense. And here we are. I couldn't feel better."

Unlike his predecessors, Day, a New Hampshire native, had no prior ties to Ohio before joining the program in 2017. That has been held against him by a fringe of an ultra-demanding fan base. After the 13-10 loss to Michigan in the regular-season finale, it wasn't just the fringe of the fan base that questioned whether he should lead the program.

But he held the team together after that loss when it could have fractured.

"He's meant everything," senior right tackle Josh Fryar said. "That's the rock of our program. Everything he does is reflected on the players and vice versa. It just goes to show his toughness and grit."

Day was a different head coach this season. He wasn't as involved in the nitty gritty of the weekly offensive game plan after hiring his mentor, Chip Kelly, as offensive coordinator. With Jim Knowles coordinating the country's top-ranked defense, Day was able to step back and take a more macro view. That allowed him to spend more time with players and get the pulse of the team.

But the pressure on Day and this team to deliver a national championship was immense. So many seniors delayed NFL careers for a season that cornerback Denzel Burke famously termed "Natty or bust" in March. The loss to Michigan denying them a chance for a Big Ten title added to the pressure. Athletic director Ross Bjork felt the need to give Day a vote of confidence the day after the Michigan game.

"I think in today's day and age, there's just so much that goes with wins and losses and social media," Day said. "People have to write articles, and there's a lot of things that are said that certainly have an effect on you and your family.

"But when you sign up for this job, that's what you sign up for. You've got to be strong enough to withstand those storms, to come out the back end.

"Now it's an even better story." ∎

Coach Ryan Day was all smiles after completing an improbable and incredible journey back from heartbreak against Michigan to claim his first national championship as a head coach.
ADAM CAIRNS/COLUMBUS DISPATCH